Saudi Arabia's Strategic Rocket Force: The Silent Service
by Norman Cigar

INTRODUCTION

The Kingdom of Saudi Arabia boasts a long-established Strategic Rocket Force (SRF). Although the SRF has developed into a significant factor in the country's military arsenal, relatively little has been made public about it over the years. To be sure, the parameters of the SRF's hardware, that is the surface-to-surface missiles (SSM), have become better known over time thanks to a number of analysts who have provided valuable insights about on-going technical developments, but even here much remains open to a good dose of conjecture. There is even less clarity about the software of the SRF, such as its role in national defense, doctrine, or force structure.

This monograph addresses the country's expanding SSM capability within the context of Riyadh's strategic thinking, overall force structure, and implications for the future. The thesis of this monograph is that recently-observed advances in Saudi Arabia's Strategic Rocket Force (Quwwat Al-Sawarikh Al-Istratijiya) and, specifically, the addition of potentially new SSM systems, are part of a long-standing continuous process intended to provide the country with a deterrent and, potentially, a warfighting capability. In effect, Riyadh has prepared the material, human, and intellectual infrastructure steadily over the years, suggesting a long-term plan to develop its SRF. A corollary is that the Saudis see SSMs as part of a cohesive package along with nuclear and space capabilities, and developments in the SRF may be an indicator supporting what some have suggested is Riyadh's intention to also acquire nuclear weapons if Iran were ever to do so.[1]

Access to information on Saudi Arabia in general is not easy to obtain, given the country's closed political system. For the SRF, Western analysts have relied largely on commercial satellite imagery and have developed valuable information, especially about the SRF's hardware. Even so, many questions are likely to remain unanswered. Moreover, all the Saudi military services have become more secretive recently, for example removing their professional journals from the web, but the SRF has always been the most reticent of the country's military services and reliable information about the SRF has always been limited. Unlike the other services, the SRF has no journal of its own (at least not one that is open to the public) and allows very little detailed coverage by the local media. Over the past few years, if anything, the SRF has become even more secretive, and is often not even included in the list of military services by Saudi sources. Yet it does remain a distinct entity, as was clear in January 2014, when it was listed as a separate service when the Minister of Defense announced a 25 per cent raise for all military personnel, ostensibly as a bonus in the fight against terrorism.[2]

In addition to glimpses that some senior Saudi figures have provided from time to time on the SRF, one must search the local media for rare bits of information and deduce certain aspects of Saudi thinking by seeing how the SRF contributes to the country's defense posture. The Saudi civilian and military media is tightly controlled by the government, and one especially sees the result in news about the SRF, with usually the same short texts and photographs (often stock photos even for graduation ceremonies) appearing in all the country's newspapers. In many ways, the Saudi media can be likened to a transmission belt, serving as an informal though semi-official vehicle presenting and promoting government policy to domestic and foreign audiences, and any information that Riyadh releases about the SRF is likely to be for the purpose of delivering a deterrence message. Of course, the thousands of blogs, tribal websites, and discussion fora in the country are less regimented than is the mainstream media, and often contain interesting information.

THE ROLE OF SAUDI ARABIA'S MISSILES: PAST, PRESENT, AND FUTURE

In order to appreciate how SSMs fit into Saudi defense, perhaps the most realistic approach is to turn the problem "inside-out," that is to evaluate the situation from the country's own perspective, in this case proceeding based on Saudi Arabia's security calculus. Key to appreciating Saudi Arabia's thinking is an analysis of what the Saudis at various levels say and an assessment of Saudi discussions within a framework of that country's strategic outlook. The present study seeks to put what information can be gleaned from the Saudi media, military writings, and blogs into a broader context of strategic culture to suggest tentative answers to at least some questions. In order to develop a clearer view of Saudi Arabia's future plans for its SRF, this study will identify and analyze that country's motivations in acquiring SSMs, the related professional military thinking, and the key milestones in the SRF's development. At the same time, in parallel to verbal evidence, of course, one must also take into consideration tangible actions related to the SRF.

The Framework of Saudi Security Culture

Perhaps the key element in understanding Saudi Arabia's strategic culture from the perspective of the country's rulers—as the identity of the state and the Al Saud ruling family tends to blur—is that of the essential need to maintain legitimacy both within the wider royal family—where competition and positioning for the future among cliques and individuals can be intense—and by the royal family within society as a whole. In Saudi Arabia's case, legitimacy consists of an aggregate collection of security, economic, religious, and symbolic legitimacy in relation to the existing system, which is embodied in the monarchy. Legitimacy, in particular, means providing for the defense of the Kingdom from foreign threats, which is also connected to another central element of legitimacy, that of providing the expected level of economic well-being, as that also depends on a safe and secure environment. Typically, the well-publicized 2009 live-fire exercise with Patriots in an anti-missile mode at the Hafr Al-Batin base complex seemed intended to fulfill that requirement, with Prince Khalid bin Sultan, then Deputy Minister of Defense, declaring openly after its completion that "a state is required to stage a display of power, since it is reassuring for any population that it has such power and that it is trained."[3]

In addition, Saudi Arabia has a self-view as the principal Arab state in the Gulf and beyond, and as having a defense mission as a regional leader. Interestingly, the SRF's logo includes an SSM superimposed over a map of the entire Arabian Peninsula, not just Saudi Arabia, and with no national borders indicated—although that is also true of the other logos of the country's defense components. (See Figure 1)

More broadly, Saudis view their country as having a special place in the Islamic world. Saudi rulers aspire to a role in protecting Muslims everywhere in the Umma (Islamic community) and benefit from the religious legitimacy that role and their protection of the Two Holy Shrines (Mecca and Medina) affords them within society and, in particular, with the key domestic religious establishment. In fact, in a clear reference to Saudi Arabia's recently-purchased SSMs, Prince Sultan in 1990 justified their acquisition by linking it to "the interrelated objectives of the defense and security of [Saudi Arabia's] holy places and of the just causes of the Arab and Islamic Umma, which constitute complementary facets … these requirements are then translated into the selection of the types of weapons that correspond to those facets."[4]

Although these are enduring interests, defense policy in Saudi Arabia is threat-based in that it responds to changing perceived threats, and considerations surrounding SSM developments have been no exception to that dynamic. In particular, the Kingdom's defense policy must address security challenges or potentially face the consequences of a loss or at least a diminution of the ruling system's legitimacy if it fails to do so. Traditionally, Saudi policymakers have operated on the basis of their perception of being surrounded by active or potential threats, which have varied over the years, as has the perceived immediacy of what the Saudis see as the two most enduring threats—Israel and Iran.

Not surprisingly, Israel has figured prominently in this respect, given its imposing military capabilities and the presence of unresolved Arab-Israeli issues. Calls for a counterweight to at least neutralize Israel's assumed nuclear weapons have long been a staple in public Saudi discourse, whether by policymakers or the country's "informed public," based on the positions articulated by opinionmakers who are allowed to speak in public, and thus presumably do not contradict official thinking. Tellingly, in a telephone conversation between Saudi Arabia's King Fahd and Egypt's President Hosni Mubarak in July 1990—which was intercepted by Iraqi Intelligence—King Fahd noted that "Israel … is now our main concern; they possess 200 nuclear warheads and 47 atom bombs and are committed to using them against us and against our Palestinian brothers."[5]

However, Saudi Arabia also saw Iran as a parallel threat, at least after the Islamic Revolution of 1979, a perception that was marked by noticeable spikes during the Iran-Iraq War (1980-88). Over the last decade, in fact, Riyadh has come to view Iran as the principal threat, due both to the latter's activism in the Arab countries and to its pursuit of a nuclear capability.

Saudi Arabia's Initial SSM Acquisition

The general outlines of the SRF's beginnings are known thanks to revelations by some of the royals involved in the original deal that saw Riyadh acquire the CSS-2[+] from China, although many of the details of the SRF's beginnings remain incomplete, especially with respect to Saudi thinking on the decision to acquire the SSMs. The motivations for Saudi Arabia's decision to acquire the SSMs at the specific time when it did can best be appreciated within the context of the country's strategic situation in the 1980s. In the wake of the Islamic Revolution and the subsequent Iran-Iraq War, Saudi Arabia felt increasingly vulnerable to potential Iranian airstrikes. At the same time, the situation in the mid-1980s at times did not look encouraging for Iraq in its war against Iran, while Israel's raids against Iraq's Osirak nuclear reactor in June 1981 and against the PLO in Tunisia in 1985 underscored Israel's ability and willingness to strike well beyond its borders.

Understandably, Riyadh was in the market for additional weaponry not only for its combat potential but also, equally importantly, for the psychological impact intended to shore up the Saudi leadership's domestic and regional legitimacy. Saudi Arabia had been shopping for SSMs since at least 1985, and Prince Khalid bin Sultan (whose father was then Minister of Defense) attributed his country's decision to seek SSMs as stemming from concerns about the "Wars of the Cities," referring to the phases of air strikes and missile exchanges by Iran and Iraq targeting each other's cities during the Iran-Iraq War.[6]

A broader motivation may have been that the Saudis viewed the SSMs as necessary for national defense overall and wanted to create a deterrent against any perceived threat in the region from whatever source. A general sense of vulnerability and the need to provide for defense during a tumultuous period in the region no doubt served as sufficient incentive to seek better weaponry. As King Fahd justified it at the time, "it is not strange at all if the Kingdom of Saudi Arabia buys defensive weapons in order to protect its religion and its country. That is the reason why the Kingdom of Saudi Arabia knocks on the doors of countries of the world in one manner or another, so that it can benefit from the type of advanced weaponry that has an impact and value."[7] According to a former SRF base commander, Prince Sultan was convinced that Saudi Arabia needed the SSMs in order to "create an arms balance in the region" and, specifically, that "Saudi Arabia was searching for a source for a powerful weapons system that would be capable of deterring an aggressor."[8]

More specifically, speaking about the acquisition of the SSMs, King Fahd highlighted the facet of legitimacy, referring to the right "to exercise our sovereignty on our own territory and to defend the

---

[+] CSS-2 is NATO designation for the Chinese produced Dong Fong-3 (DF-3) intermediate range, surface-based, liquid propellant, single warhead ballistic missile, with a payload of 2,000kg and a range of 2,500 km. (*IHS Jane's* "Strategic Weapons Systems: DF-3 (CSS-2)" last updated 7 May 2014).

nation and the holy places of all Muslims."[9] In particular, Saudi Arabia's acquisition of SSMs dovetailed with an enduring desire by the Saudi leadership to portray itself as active and able to provide for the country's own defense (however exaggerated such a portrayal might be), mostly for domestic and regional audiences, and was intended to bolster the Saudi regime's legitimacy, as Prince Khalid suggested. In his view, "I assume that King Fahd decided that we needed a weapon to improve the morale of our armed services and our people."[10] According to a retired senior Saudi military officer, when a visiting senior U.S. official had advised Prince Sultan to rely on the United States for its defense, the latter had replied that "The Kingdom of Saudi Arabia relies only on God and on the arms of its sons for its security."[11]

It is easy to appreciate why SSMs even as a stand-alone conventional system would have been desirable from a Saudi point of view. The Saudis have continued to view SSMs as an effective and cost-effective weapon system, with one senior officer highlighting SSMs' speed, range, accuracy, the difficulty in defending against them, their relative lower cost compared to airpower, and "the ability to carry warheads with immense destructive power and great lethality, especially nuclear and chemical ones."[12] One Saudi commentator highlighted not only the significance of SSMs in national defense but also that, in his view, as a relative inexpensive solution, arguing that "Today, one of the basic foundations of defensive deterrence is that of ballistic missiles, thanks to their accuracy, especially when used in combination with satellite technology; and, both these systems are not expensive and are relatively easily available."[13] Another analyst writing in a Saudi military journal— albeit addressing in generic terms SSMs in the Middle East as a whole—clearly saw as one of their attractions that they could be a force multiplier, since "they compensate for human and material deficiencies in military force structures."[14]

What catalyzed the Saudis to seek SSMs specifically from China? The United States had rejected Saudi requests to buy Lance missiles (which only have a 50 mile range) in 1979. Furthermore, while the sale of the F-15 was approved in 1978, this did not include the version with a ground attack capability, while Riyadh had received approval for the AWACS aircraft in 1981 only after a bruising public struggle. A government official and eventually a member of the country's Shura (Consultative Council) provided an account of what was apparently the immediate catalyst for the deal with China. According to this source, Prince Bandar bin Sultan (then-Saudi ambassador to Washington), had told him that King Fahd had made the decision to seek SSMs from China following the monarch's visit to the White House in February 1985, when he had been pressured intensively to support a peace plan for the Palestinians which he felt was heavily biased in favor of Israel, and that he specifically wanted to send a message to the United States that Saudi Arabia's decisionmaking was independent.[15] By approaching China, then probably the only country able and willing to provide SSMs to Riyadh, the latter also was able to make a statement about its independence, as Prince Sultan affirmed that Saudi Arabia was "free to choose the sources of supply depending on the type and capability of weapon."[16] Likewise, King Fahd himself stressed that "the Kingdom of Saudi Arabia is free to buy weaponry from anyone it believes provides the quality weapons which the Kingdom of Saudi Arabia believes it needs."[17] Again, when asked by a Kuwaiti newspaper why Saudi Arabia had purchased the SSMs from China even though Riyadh was western-oriented, King Fahd had noted that "Our national interests direct our country's orientation; we are not with anyone but with our own interests."[18]

One of the additional attractions of dealing with China in the initial SSM purchase was that country's ability to maintain operational security and discretion, which contrasted to the often embarrassing public debates surrounding Saudi arms requests in the United States. Saudi appreciation on this score was long-lasting and in 2010 King Abd-Allah told the Chinese ambassador that Saudi Arabia wanted to rely more on China for military equipment, "especially since China maintained secrecy when it sold the long-range CSS-2 missiles to the Saudi Armed Forces."[19]

In the event, once the decision had been made, Saudi Arabia quickly dispatched in secret a delegation of three princes, Prince Khalid (then Commander of the Air Defense), his brother Prince Bandar, and Prince Abd-Allah bin Faysal, who completed the negotiations with China to acquire the SSMs in the course of several visits. According to the U.S. media, the original Sino-Saudi SSM deal for the CSS-2s was sealed by July 1985.[20] To allay any suspicions, the Saudis used deception, telling the United States that the new construction for the SSM facilities was for an ammunition depot.[21] On the other hand, Prince Khalid claims that the Americans had detected the Saudis being trained in China and the construction of the new SSM base, but had waited until the project was nearly complete before protesting.[22]

Imagery analysis in early March 1988 had alerted the United States as to the presence of the SSMs (which apparently had begun to arrive that January) and Washington raised strong objections. According to Saudi sources, the United States at the time allegedly requested that Saudi Arabia dismantle and return the SSMs or at least allow U.S. officials to inspect them.[23] The Saudis sharply rejected all such pressure. In Riyadh, according to Prince Khalid, King Fahd was angered by the U.S. ambassador's demarche requesting permission to inspect the SSMs, and the ambassador had to be recalled soon thereafter.[24] Similarly, in Washington, according to another of Prince Sultan's sons, Faysal, U.S. officials also pressured his father—then in the United States for knee surgery—to grant access to the SSMs. Prince Sultan had refused, unless Israel also agreed to have its arsenals inspected, which the Saudis knew was a non-starter.[25] Moreover, Prince Sultan added, Saudi Arabia had bought the SSMs with its own money, whereas Israel bought its weapons with U.S. money and support.

At the time, senior Saudi officials repeatedly offered assurances that the newly-acquired SSMs did not and would not be linked to weapons of mass destruction (WMD). King Fahd, for example, told a local audience that "we reassured anyone who asked us that the [SSMs] really do not carry nuclear or chemical warheads; rather, they are only defensive missiles and nothing else."[26] Likewise, an unnamed Saudi "official source" informed the local media that foreign press reports to the effect that the newly-acquired CSS-2s were nuclear-capable had "no basis in fact and the Kingdom denies that categorically."[27] Prince Sultan, for his part, stressed that although "the Kingdom of Saudi Arabia is capable of acquiring and producing nuclear weapons, it is common knowledge that the Kingdom was among the first to call for a nuclear weapons-free Middle East."[28] Moreover, Prince Bandar claimed that Riyadh had paid the Chinese to modify the CSS-2 to carry a conventional warhead.[29]

Mobilizing National Pride and Safeguarding Legitimacy

In most countries, SSMs are equated to national progress, modernity, and national pride, as well as being a lethal weapon. The Saudi government and the country's civilian and military media have not only monitored Iranian and Israeli arms developments closely, but have also publicized such developments routinely, and often in dire terms, over the past decade, probably as a way to sensitize the Saudi and regional publics to the threat. (See Figure 2)

The Saudi government may also have seen this approach as an effective method to mobilize public and military support at home for the ruling system and for such regional initiatives as Riyadh's project for a unified Gulf Cooperation Council (GCC) under its aegis. At the same time, the Saudi government must be seen as effective in providing for defense against such publicized threats and, insofar as possible, with local capabilities rather than depending on non-Muslims.

Appealing to national pride clearly has also been a related factor in showcasing Saudi Arabia's SSM capabilities. Tellingly, the entrance of the Saudi Ministry of Defense in Riyadh is formed by an arch of two missiles. Yet the need for publicity has had to be balanced with the requirements for operational security, and Riyadh has also taken satisfaction in its ability to maintain a significant degree of secrecy about its SSM program. Thus, shortly after news of the SSM's presence was made public by the United States in 1988, then-Minister of Defense Prince Sultan noted with evident delight that foreign intelligence services had not detected the SSMs for almost two years after the system's original delivery. He added that "we are proud that not a single one of the Saudi youths—our sons the officers, technicians, and experts who received training on the SSMs and who deployed them in their country—revealed anything about them. They did not give away the secret and there were no leaks."[30] As the SRF's commander, Staff Major General Jar-Allah al-Awit, still boasted in 2010, "the creation of this force took place in silence, and it became a giant and carried out its training in secret."[31]

However, being perceived as doing nothing can also have its costs for the Saudi government and, over the years, the media has been allowed to increase its coverage of the SRF—although still within very limited bounds—and to boast, no doubt in order to support deterrence and to mobilize public support which could translate into regime legitimacy. For example, on the occasion of the inauguration of new construction at Base 511 at Al-Hariq in 1999, an editorial in the Saudi press about the SSMs waxed that the SSMs are "a capable deterrent force against anyone who considers violating the Land of the Two Holy Shrines, its riches, people, and its citizens' achievements."[32]

Likewise, at the ceremony of the opening of the SRF's new headquarters in 2010, in the presence of the then-Deputy Minister of Defense Prince Khalid, the SRF commander, Staff Major General Jar-Allah al-Awit, said that the Saudi leadership "understood … the important role this type of weaponry [i.e. SSMs] plays in deterring any threat to this country's holy places and national assets."[33] (See Figure 3)

Understandably anxious to promote his own service, in 2010 the commander of the SRF also announced that SSMs had become "one of the most important means by which countries achieve stability and deterrence" and assured audiences that Saudi Arabia "has the necessary infrastructure and the human resources enabling it to fully achieve the defensive deterrent force that the Kingdom requires."[34] And, he also made a case that the SRF was a development engine for the entire nation, especially for the civilian population in the areas surrounding the SRF bases.[35] In that context, an editorial reinforced the regime's image by portraying the SSMs as "an example of what our visionary leadership offers to this country's children, within a cohesive strategy in which this country's citizens are at its heart."[36]

Missiles stir the popular imagination, being linked to national progress as well as seen as a reason for national pride, as is evident in Saudi fora and in readers' comments to online versions of local newspapers. And, moreover, Saudis often think that even more could be done, as a poster on the King Saud University forum in 2006 suggested. This blogger praised Pakistan's missile tests, contrasting that with what he called "backwardness in our intellectual production," and bemoaned the fact that in Saudi Arabia websites about the making of rockets are censored, stressing the importance of amateur rocket clubs in the West.[37] Even Saudi clerics often imbued the acquisition of SSMs or nuclear weapons with a spiritual cachet as a support for the Umma's defense. This religious cachet was mixed with a sense of emotional empowerment in what they saw as needed in order to attain the world's respect. For example, well-known cleric A'id al-Qarni, in an article that quickly went viral, accused the West of seeking to prevent others from acquiring advanced military technology such as SSMs because the West "knows that whoever rules the world and controls its resources needs to have dominating power and clear supremacy."[38] And, he put the need to arm into religious terms, quoting the Quran's injunction to prepare against enemies, and noted that "manufacturing a missile is more useful than one hundred celebratory festivities."[39]

Saudi Operational Thinking

Understanding Saudi operational thinking with respect to the SSMs and broader strategy is not easy, as no Saudi doctrinal document on SSMs has ever appeared in public, and probably does not exist, while discussions about strategic issues are usually tightly controlled. Even well-placed Saudis may find official thinking on strategy unclear and sometimes have complained, even if obliquely, about the lack of clarity of such deliberations. For example, a senior planning official in the Ministry of Defense, calling for the participation of think tanks and experts in the formulation of strategy, rued that "economic, political, and security strategies are not clear, since they remain in the minds of senior men in the government; they are like senior officers who do not let junior employees in on them or in formulating them."[40] Likewise, a frustrated senior Air Defense Forces officer spoke of the lack of clear guidance for defense planning, noting that "What is needed is transparency and clarity by other parts of the government with respect to any information needed to draft strategy; there is a need to overcome the resistance by some authorities about stating clearly what the assumed security threats are."[41] As he noted, "there is no cohesive written military strategy to provide clearly the broad outlines for the military leadership in charge."[42]

Nevertheless, assumptions must guide thinking about the employment of the country's SSMs. What one has to work with in this arena are general Saudi policy guidelines and assumptions, the national strategic culture, and enduring national interests, supplemented by occasional official statements and discussions in the military and civilian media, although here too, one cannot expect a clear translation of policy into concepts and doctrine. One must rely on a process of deduction, based on the country's previous experience where SSMs have played a role and on the available Saudi military literature, which often discusses issues related to SSMs in general terms or focuses on the experience of other countries. Saudi Arabia has used its SSMs on several occasions, at least as a deterrent, and looking at past practice may provide some indications of Saudi thinking and potential future behavior.

The Saudi Conceptualization of Deterrence

Saudi Arabia has used its SSMs in a deterrent mode at least three times: against any Israeli strike after the SSMs were publicized in 1988, that same year against Iran, and against Iraq in 1990-91 following the latter's invasion of Kuwait and during the ensuing Gulf War.

Riyadh saw its initial SSMs in and of themselves as an element primarily of deterrence, and Prince Khalid noted the SSMs' primary role was as "a weapon which would make an enemy think twice before attacking us," while the Saudis would rely on camouflage and dispersion to retain a second-strike capability.[43] Deterrence has remained a guiding pillar of Saudi strategic thinking. As a senior Saudi officer put it in 2010, "Ballistic missiles are considered one of the instruments of armed conflict in our age, given the deterrent capability they provide, so that all countries have been compelled to seek them in order to achieve national security."[44] To some extent, the Saudis view deterrence in terms of a "fleet-in-being," with a system's presence sufficient to achieve a level of deterrence. As the Commander of the SRF, Staff Major General Jar-Allah al-Awit, has claimed, the SRF's "birth created fear and by its very existence it achieved deterrence."[45]

The Saudis seem to prefer deterrence based on a policy of ambiguity, and have shown admiration openly in their writings for Israel's own policy on that score. But, of course, a weapon of whose existence others are not aware, or at least suspect, cannot serve as a deterrent or threat, as the Saudis clearly recognized. As Prince Bandar put it, the intent was to make the CSS-2s acquired from China public, for "that was the real value of the weapon; if no one knew about it, it could scarcely be a deterrent."[46] But, that had to be done at the right time. Specifically, the Saudis had decided that they would reveal the existence of their new SSMs once the entire system was operational, but wanted to select when to reveal their new SSM deterrent for, as Prince Bandar noted with respect to that, "timing is everything."[47] According to Prince Khalid, the expected date that the SSMs might be detected was by February 1989, but if that had not occurred by June 1989 then Saudi Arabia would make them public.[48] The plan was for Prince Sultan to then hold a press conference at which he would announce that King Fahd had visited the SSM force. According to Prince Bandar, by the time the United States became aware of the new SSMs only one-half the SSMs purchased had arrived in-country.[49] However, in retrospect, the Saudis might well have moved up that planning date—even if the SSM force was not yet completely ready, and even if the United States had not detected the SSMs as it did in March 1988—in order to counter the Iranian threat, as the "War of the Cities," involving exchanges of missiles between the two neighboring belligerents, intensified in March-April 1988.

The Israelis, as one might have imagined, were displeased by the new developments in neighboring Saudi Arabia. Accompanying Premier Itzhak Shamir on a visit to the United States in March 1988, one of his aides told the media that Israel might take action unilaterally against Saudi Arabia's SSMs, as "Israel has acquired a reputation of not waiting until a potential danger becomes actual."[50] Moreover, there were also reports of practice bombing runs by the Israel Air Force, either as preparation for an attack or to intimidate Saudi Arabia.[51]

Riyadh became alarmed about a possible Israeli strike. Although not mentioning the new missiles directly, Saudi Arabia's King Fahd condemned Israeli threats and declared that "Saudi Arabia will continue to carry through its legitimate defensive programs," warning that "we are prepared to defend our holy places."[52] The Saudi media underlined and amplified the King's message of deterrence, as one press editorial warned that "When the Kingdom is intent on building up its independent power and might, it does so, so that this will be a force for peace and security that will deter others and prevent them from even thinking of attempting aggression. If they do do so, [Saudi Arabia] is able, God willing, to defend the entire country and to protect the holy places and to repay the aggressors' plots forcefully."[53] A few days later, King Fahd, in an interview, once again focused on the new SSMs, and voiced a threat that Saudi Arabia "is not prepared to stand by idly to anyone who attacks it, [and will] use any available means. Thank God, we have weapons that I can say are if not superior to the weapons found in the rest of the region at least equal to them, whether aircraft or other weapons."[54]

According to the then-Minister of Defense Prince Sultan, in the wake of the Israeli threats, Saudi Arabia had informed the United States that it would respond with all means to any Israeli attack and had placed its forces on full alert, thereby also practicing indirect deterrence.[55] In effect, Prince Bandar, then-Saudi ambassador in Washington, confirmed that he had warned the U.S. government that if Israel struck Saudi Arabia, the latter would have to retaliate, including by using its SSMs, probably expecting Washington—anxious to avoid an armed confrontation in the Middle East—to then pressure Israel to desist.[56] At the same time, according to Prince Bandar, "Saudi Arabia asked the United States to send a discreet message to Israel that the CSS-2 would not be directed against Israel."[57] Probably, U.S. calls on Tel Aviv for restraint, as well as the latter's less alarmist reinterpretation of the threat, had more to do with deterring Israel than the prospect of Saudi retaliation.[58]

Shortly thereafter, when Riyadh severed relations with Iran, accusing the latter of subversion, and addressing specifically the on-going Iran-Iraq War, King Fahd hinted publicly that the country's new SSM "will be used in case of any threats against our country ... if we are obliged to use our defensive power, watch out."[59] In the context of the escalation of the missile exchanges as part of the "War of the Cities" between the two belligerents and the venue of a Kuwaiti newspaper for the interview, the intended recipient of King Fahd's message was clearly Iran. However, Riyadh may have been brandishing its SSM deterrent even though its missiles may not yet have been fully operational.[60] Although other sources suggested that the Saudi SSMs did not become fully operational until considerably later, in mid-1990, the latter date may have referred to the force as a whole.[61]

Deterrence and Warfighting

At the same time, Saudi military thinkers have shown they are fully aware that an effective deterrent also requires credibility that the capability would be used and that deterrence and warfighting exist in tandem. As a study in a Saudi military journal stressed, "the decisive factor today, as it has been throughout history, is the ability to use a weapon." It is this factor which "must constitute a deterrent to the leadership in Tehran in order to prevent that leadership from embarking on a military venture whose outcome is uncertain or to prevent it from igniting an armed conflict whose cost exceeds the value of that war."[62] In that respect, according to the same author, "the GCC states' arsenals of arms and the ability to use them is in favor of the Gulf states more than in Iran's favor, and that must constitute a deterrent factor to Tehran's leadership."[63] Prince Khalid, likewise, saw in the SSMs an effective weapon for a counterattack, what he called the ability to "demoralize the enemy by delivering a painful and decisive blow."[64]

During the Gulf War, Riyadh wielded its recently-acquired SSM capability in a deterrent mode, communicating with both clear and veiled messages directed at Saddam Hussein. For example, the Minister of Defense, Prince Sultan, warned in September 1990 that if Iraq resorted to chemical weapons, "we are able, first of all, to thwart that before it happens, but that will make us use the fearful weapons we possess, including missiles that are able to reach the depths of Iraq. We possess the means to cause destruction, as Saddam Hussein well knows, and we all hope that we will not get to that point and I still appeal in the name of peace."[65] The Saudi press coverage of that speech, moreover, stressed the Saudi missile capability aspect. Apart from the intent to deter the Iraqis, such saber-rattling no doubt was also meant to reassure jittery domestic audiences who especially feared an Iraqi chemical attack. As Prince Khalid (at the time Commander of the Combined Forces) had noted a few days earlier in a press conference when discussing retaliation for any Iraqi attack chemical attack, "We have the means to thwart [Saddam's] plans, and I give assurances to our dear population in order that they may put their minds at rest, since everything has been thought out."[66]

Subsequent events, however, showed that Saudi Arabia was also willing to use its SSMs as a conventional warfighting weapon if deterrence failed. Prince Khalid maintained that Saudi Arabia would have launched only as a last resort, "only if all other available weapons had been used … and if this was absolutely vital and unavoidable."[67] Earlier, Saudi leaders had focused on Iraq's use of unconventional weapons as the threshold that would induce Riyadh to launch its SSMs. In fact, as Prince Khalid later confided, "we had … prepared an appropriate response that would have taught [Saddam Hussein] a lesson" had the latter decided to launch SSMs with chemical or biological warheads—as Prince Khalid said the Saudis fully expected.[68] It was not only a need to respond to material damage that Iraqi SSMs might cause but perhaps also an even greater need to be seen to be doing something in order to bolster the government's domestic legitimacy. Significantly, Prince Khalid noted in this respect that "we all know that these [Iraqi] missiles had a greater psychological than destructive impact."[69]

As it was, the conventionally-armed Iraqi Scuds caused only negligible damage and casualties. However, Riyadh came close to using its SSMs, and one may posit that if an Iraqi Scud—even if only a conventionally-armed one—had made a lucky hit and struck a sensitive target—a crowded shopping mall, oil facilities, a royal palace—and caused many casualties, the Saudis might have felt compelled to respond in kind. Riyadh, in fact, changed its previously-declared red-line, which had been Iraq's use of chemical weapons, since the launch threshold was apparently almost reached even though Iraq remained at the conventional level. According to Prince Khalid, "the Saudi SSMs were ready and aimed at several military targets … I remember that on one occasion the order was given for operational readiness to launch a concentrated volley against one of the targets. All that was needed was the actual order to fire."[70] Elsewhere, he designated the intended targets more generally as "the key Iraqi sites," perhaps indicating a broader target list beyond just military locations.[71] Given the inaccuracy of the CSS-2, such targets would have had to be of large size— perhaps a military base or government complex—although even Baghdad may not have been excluded if the situation had deteriorated to an unacceptable level. Prince Khalid notes that it was he who had issued that order, that the SSMs were massed, and that all preparations to launch were in place apart from inserting the liquid fuel.[72] However, as Prince Khalid puts it, "Thanks to the wisdom, humanitarianism, and concern for the welfare of the Iraqi people, the supreme commander [King Fahd] ordered at the last minute not to launch."[73] Elsewhere, however, Prince Khalid claims that the decision not to fire was based on a desire not to escalate and to retain, instead, the SSMs as a last resort.[74] Besides, he adds, the Coalition was already providing "an adequate response" for the moment.

Although one cannot determine the effect the Saudi SSMs had on either Israeli or Iraqi decision-making, as Iraq did launch at least conventionally-armed Scud missiles against Saudi Arabia, according to Prince Khalid, Saudi leaders believed that their deterrence had been successful.[75] Israel did not attack the SSMs and Iran did not launch its missiles against Saudi Arabia in 1988 and, presumably, in the case of the Gulf War, the measure of success was in preventing Iraq's use of chemical weapons. However, in the cases of Israel, Iran, and Iraq, other extraneous factors (such as U.S. pressure and threats or other political considerations) very likely were decisive in achieving the deterrent results rather than the Saudi SSMs themselves.

In a more recent episode, Riyadh apparently made no public mention of its SSMs for deterrence when—during a period of heightened bilateral tension revolving around Saudi aid to the Syrian rebels engaged against the Moscow-backed Asad regime—a senior Russian Air Force officer was reported to have made a threat in June 2013 to strike Saudi Arabia. The unnamed officer reminded his audience that there were already long-standing operational plans for such an option and that Moscow has that capability.[76] The mainstream Saudi media ignored the threat, although a few of the electronic newspapers with limited readerships reproduced foreign reports of that news.[77] Even the average Saudi must have been aware of the event thanks to spread of the news on the internet by most of the newspapers in the Arab world and by Arabic-language satellite news channels, such as CNN Arabic and Microsoft's MSN Arabic.[78] Saudi tribal news outlets and websites also reproduced these reports.[79] Saudi bloggers in general reacted defiantly against such threats, as reported in the local electronic press.[80] Given the disparity in the power between Russia and Saudi Arabia, the latter probably had no desire to draw attention to the threat or to escalate tensions with Moscow. What is more, as a Saudi commentator suggested, although considerably later, he had not viewed this as "a serious threat requiring taking cautionary measures," and that it may not have been viewed in Riyadh as a realistic threat.[81]

Considering Future Employment

The SRF's stated mission in general terms, according to the Commander of the SRF, Staff Major General Jar-Allah al-Alwit, remains "the security and defense of the nation and the building of a deterrent force to protect the nation's holy places and achievements."[82] Analysts in the Saudi military media have continued to focus on the effectiveness of SSMs for deterrence, as one did when he noted that "Surface-to-surface ballistic missiles are one of the key elements used as a deterrent force, and possessing a missile force of this type is considered one of the most important guarantees to deter an enemy and to preserve stability."[83] While the reports of subsequent purchases of SSMs can also be viewed in that perspective, more recently, as will be seen below, Saudi analysts and commentators have focused increasingly on nuclear weapons in that deterrent role, with SSMs playing a key supporting role as a delivery system.

As in the past, within the context of Saudi Arabia's enduring security culture, the focus of defense is likely to remain on deterrence, although, as noted, that entails developing a credible warfighting capability and a perceived willingness to use it. In an editorial in a Saudi-owned newspaper, the former director of Iraq's Military Intelligence, Lieutenant General Wafiq al-Samarra'i, advised that "the Gulf" might need SSMs to not only deter but to also counterattack, for simply "defensive wars cannot bring victory."[84] The Saudi consensus on the concept of deterrence clearly has contained a warfighting component. As one commentator on defense issues noted, "the concept of strategic deterrence is an offensive military concept, meaning that if I am subjected to an attack by the other side then my response will not be to attempt to repel that attack but rather to mount an equivalent attack to the same or a greater degree of punishment on the other side."[85] An unspoken but no doubt key intent of the Patriot demonstration in 2009 was the implication that Saudi Arabia could protect its own SSM force for a second strike. That is, by showing that it could shoot down most incoming missiles, potential adversaries would see that they could not destroy Saudi Arabia's entire SSM force and that the latter would thus have sufficient SSMs left to retaliate.

Moreover, one cannot exclude that the Saudis might also consider a preemptive strike with their own SSMs if they became convinced that an adversary intended to launch a first strike.

But, have the SSMs ever been test-fired? There is no information about that in the public domain. However, it would make sense that at some time the SRF has done so, not only for operational training but simply to check on the SSMs' readiness. There have been possible suggestions to that effect from time to time. For example, when then-Deputy Defense Minister, Prince Abd al-Rahman, visited Base 522 in June 2000, he witnessed what media accounts called "a practical application for missiles."[86] In June 2005, Prince Abd al-Rahman, as part of the graduating ceremony at the SRF School at Base 522, again was reported to also have witnessed an unspecified "practical application" at the operational wing, performed by the graduating class.[87] The 2009 Patriot exercise apparently was a force-on-force event, but it is not at all clear what that actually involved and whether any Saudi SSMs were also launched, although a report in an official Saudi newspaper noted that "the operational exercise culminated with the Patriot countering ballistic missiles."[88]

Saudi Arabia will still face a threat from Iran whether or not the latter acquires a nuclear capability. For the Saudis, even the development of their own nuclear sector would still mean the need for a robust conventional capability at every level. This would forestall placing Saudi Arabia in an unenviable position in the future—should it decide to acquire nuclear weapons—where nuclear weapons would be the only remaining military option in case of a military conflict with Iran if it could not match Iran at lower levels of force. One of the lessons a Saudi scholar highlighted from the U.S. experience was that of "developing conventional military capabilities in order to be able to engage in a limited war without having recourse to using WMD."[89] Significantly, a $30 billion U.S.-Saudi arms deal was announced in December 2011 for conventional military equipment intended not only to deter Iran at present but, apparently, also as a means to make Iran realize that it could not gain any advantage by escalating to the use of more lethal weapons in the future—that is, "escalation dominance"[+]—by implying that Riyadh could respond effectively at every level of force. SSMs, of course, would retain their conventional deterrent and warfighting role even in a nuclear environment, and one analyst in a Saudi military journal saw SSMs as a step on the escalation ladder, a system whose use would serve "as a penultimate card preceding the use of nuclear weapons."[90]

The converse, a capability to defend against enemy SSMs, also enhances one's own SSM-based deterrence, as it reduces the impact of an enemy strike, including against the home country's SSM force. Although Prince Khalid denied that Saudi Arabia wanted to send a message to anyone in conjunction with the 2009 live-fire exercise with the anti-missile Patriot system, the head of the Control and Exercise Committee, Major General Salih Abd al-Rahman al-Suqayri, nevertheless underlined the success of the exercise in defending against incoming SSMs, clearly a reference to such threats from countries in the region.[91]

[+] "Escalation dominance" was a technical term prevalent during the Cold War. That is, the U.S. was concerned that it would be prevented from being able to escalate because the Soviets would still have had superiority at each level (conventional, tactical nuclear weapons, and strategic nuclear weapons).

DEVELOPING THE STRATEGIC ROCKET FORCE

The evident continuity in the SRF's development suggests a long-term vision, although one responding to a shifting threat environment. The Saudi government certainly appears to have invested heavily in the SRF over the years and, typically, Prince Sultan told an SRF graduating class in 1992 that they were "the apple of our eyes."[92]

The SRF formally came into existence on 8 September 1986 by royal decree. In organizational terms, the SRF holds a special position, since it is considered a "strategic force," as Prince Khalid told the local press in 2007.[93] It is the fifth service of the Saudi military, although far smaller than the other four, and remains a separate service, for example fielding its own team for the military's Quran memorization tournament and for an unspecified athletic competition.[94] However, according to a blogger who is in the SRF, the latter is tied to Air Defense in financial affairs. The commander of the SRF seemed to imply that the Minister of Defense and the Deputy Minister of Defense hold operational command and control over the SRF, as he noted that the latter would carry out its mission "under the guidance of His Highness the Prince, the Minister of Defense, and of his deputy in order to achieve the desired objective."[95] As is true with the other military services, the royal family keeps effective control of the SRF tightly in its hands and, as is common practice, has not refrained from bypassing the formal chain of command to exercise control. According to an officer who had been the base commander at Al-Sulayyil Base for eight years, the Minister of Defense Prince Sultan was said to have had frequent direct hands-on involvement with the base, bypassing the Commander of the SRF. According to that source, "the situation required direct decisions and orders from his gracious highness."[96] In fact, Prince Sultan had told him that should there be any issues, "Just contact me directly, and if any issue arises involving you, I will contact you directly."[97]

Developing the SRF's Software

Saudi Arabia has been engaged in a long-term development of what one can term the SRF's software, i.e. those material and human elements needed to operate a missile force. This development strongly suggests a planned long-term expansion of the SRF's size and a parallel increase in the SRF's importance in the country's defense strategy. Although this process can be tracked throughout the 1990s, it appears to have gained momentum over the last decade as perceptions of the regional threat have grown.

Even just the publicly-announced infrastructure facilities indicate that considerable money and attention have been invested in the SRF, and into its accompanying qualitative and quantitative development. Hyperbole and ingratiation aside, there is an element of truth when the SRF leadership has spoken of the "unlimited support" it has received from the national leadership.[98] In an initial construction phase, for example, in 1992 Prince Sultan presided over the opening of the SRF School and Training Center at Base 522 at Al-Sulayyil.[99] In December 1999, then-Crown Prince Abd-Allah inaugurated a tactical facility, not further identified, and a residential complex at Base 511 at Al-Hariq.[100] The Kuwait News Agency elaborated that these new facilities included living quarters for all ranks of military personnel, a power plant, a water purification facility, and a clinic.[101] In June 2000, Deputy Minister of Defense Prince Abd al-Rahman inaugurated a recreational park in Wadi Al-Dawasir for Al-Sulayyil Base with such amenities as a prayer area and facilities for fishing, as well as six artificial lakes said to be intended for the evaporation of surplus water after its purification on base, and a new road linking Wadi Al-Dawasir to central Najd.[102] The following year, Prince Abd al-Rahman opened another 40 km-long road linking Al-Sulayyil Base with the town of Al-Daliya, as well as wells and a park in the area, all at his personal expense.[103] Another building phase began in the mid-2000s, no doubt reflecting the heightened tensions in the region. By 2010, a new SRF headquarters opened in Riyadh.[104] In 2011, a new Training Center was inaugurated at Al-Sulayyil Base.[105] In January 2013, additional offices and activity facilities were opened at Al-Hariq Base.[106]

==

Today, one can identify at least five SSM-related facilities, based on imagery, other intelligence, and the Saudi media and blogs.

- SSM Base 522 or Al-Sulayyil Base and Training Center (also called Wadi Al-Dawasir), 450 km southwest of Riyadh
- SSM Base 511or Al-Hariq Base (also called Al-Jufayr and Al-Huta), 115 km south of Riyadh
- SSM Base at Al-Watah (also called Al-Shamli and Al-Dawadimi), 201 km southwest of Riyadh
- SRF Headquarters, Riyadh
- Al-Ta'if, Support and maintenance facility

Saudi sources sometimes also use the designations 533, 544 and 566 for some of the SRF facilities, although it is not clear to which facility each number refers.

==

Of course, in tandem with the material expansion, there has also been an expansion of the human sector. Initially, technical support and very probably the actual operational handling of the SSMs was in the hands of Chinese advisers, and one can assume reasonably that it was Chinese personnel who conducted the operational functions related to the new SSMs when a launch was contemplated in 1988, given the short lead-time between purchase and delivery and the inability to have trained Saudi personnel by that time. A Chinese presence may well have continued for many years thereafter, as suggested by the fact that as late as 2010 the King awarded one of the country's highest decorations to the Chinese head of the Joint Military Committee in recognition for "strengthening friendship and cooperation."[107] Since the ceremony was hosted by Saudi Arabia's SRF, the event was clearly in connection with China's support of the SSM program. (See Figure 4)

It is hard to tell how many Chinese personnel were involved and for how long. According to a Saudi media source, at one time there had been 1000 Chinese trainers and technicians as part of the program.[108] In 1997, according to the Commander of the SRF, there were said to be 150 to 300 Chinese personnel working with the SSMs.[109] One Saudi commentator to a press story claimed in 2013 that Chinese SSM advisers were still present, disguised as civil defense personnel.[110] It is very likely that there is still a substantial foreign technical presence (from whatever country) with this program, if Saudi Arabia's experience of requiring foreign support for virtually all its advanced conventional systems is any indicator, and this dependence has likely increased if the reports of the new SSM systems are confirmed.

At first, Saudi personnel in the SRF would have had to be drawn from the other existing military services.[111] Since then, Saudi military and civilian personnel have been trained to undertake many of the necessary functions. By 2010, the commander of the SRF, Staff Major General al-Awit, revealed that the number of military and civilian personnel serving in the SRF now numbered "in the thousands."[112] Indicative of the SRF's recent growth, in 2011 the Ministry of Defense placed ads in the local media in quest for additional off-base housing in areas surrounding the base at Al-Hariq.[113]

Recruitment, based on some of the names of those in the senior ranks, seems to follow a pattern of preference for tribal individuals, as is true for much of the Saudi military, at least for the non-technical positions. For the past few years, the yearly recruitment cycle has been publicized in the local media, with the SRF seeking candidates at all levels, with initial rank depending on educational experience, up to captain for those with a university degree. Reflecting the sensitive nature of the service, a candidate's spouse cannot be a foreigner. Officers destined for the SRF are educated at the country's Air Defense Academy in Al-Ta'if.[114] New enlisted recruits go through a three-month basic course at the SRF School at Al-Sulayyil Base, followed by a six-month technical course for those doing technical work. New officers and warrant officers also attend a course lasting almost a year in the SRF School. (See Figure 5) The same school also provides specialized training and students can also attend other schools for technical courses, such as the national Institute for Military Geography and Terrain. Some officers also finish a four-month technical course at the civilian Technical College in the town of Wadi Al-Dawasir, near Al-Sulayyil.[115]

Despite the government's unstinting support, building esprit de corps in the SRF may be difficult, as it no doubt has to compete with the government and private civilian sectors for technically competent personnel who are vital for a force such as the SRF, despite the overall shortage of job opportunities in the country even for educated Saudis. Drawbacks for the SRF may include that its operational bases are located in isolated, underdeveloped, areas, and one is almost guaranteed not to be stationed in a city, to which most Saudi youth aspire, as some Saudi forum posters have noted. And, instead, bloggers have discussed as preferable working for a civilian firm in some more attractive urban location such as Jeddah. Again in fora, students have complained that the technical coursework in the SRF is more difficult than at a university and that, in addition, students have to perform administrative and military duties while studying.[116] Moreover, the SRF prides itself on its ability to remain in the shadows and there is a high degree of secrecy, with little publicity, no festivals, professional journal, or celebrations on the anniversary of its founding, as there are for the other services, or, until recently, even a parade. However, according to discussions in multiple Saudi fora, as far as compensation goes, entry-level salaries for personnel in the SRF are reportedly higher than for those in the country's Land Force and promotions more rapid.

Developing the SRF's Hardware

Developments in the SRF's hardware—the SSMs themselves—have also been difficult to document. The Israeli press provided the first substantive analysis of the Saudis SSMs in 2002, based on satellite imagery that included the publication of the annotated imagery of one of the bases.[117] Not surprisingly, at least by the late 1990s, Saudi Arabia was looking to update its SSM arsenal, as the Commander of the SRF, Lieutenant General Salih al-Muhayya, told an interviewer in 1997 that his country was "assessing the replacement or modernization" of its aging CSS-2 SSMs.[118]

In 2010, based on his work in the U.S. intelligence community, former analyst Jonathan Scherck, claimed that perhaps as early as 2003 Saudi Arabia had begun acquiring the CSS-5 from China.[119] While having a shorter range than the liquid-fuel CSS-2, the CSS-5 is more accurate and is propelled by solid fuel, making a launch quicker and less complicated. In July 2013, again based on satellite imagery, the London-based *Jane's Defence Weekly* revealed that Saudi Arabia had SSMs at a previously-unreported base at Al-Watah, targeted at Iran and Israel, although assuming the SSMs to be the CSS-2s.[120] However, nonproliferation expert Jeffrey Lewis, in an insightful commentary in the wake of a tantalizing photo appearing in the Saudi media in May 2013, speculated that the Saudi missile inventory included the CSS-5.[121] The country's official news agency, in effect, had released a photograph to the Saudi media showing models of three different missiles presented by the SRF as a gift to the visiting Deputy Minister of Defense Prince Fahd bin Abd-Allah. (See Figure 6)

The message was that Saudi Arabia now also had potentially two SSMs other than the CSS-2, or at least two versions of an additional SSM type including, perhaps, the nuclear-capable solid-fuel-propelled Shaheen II from Pakistan, a country with which Riyadh has had a long-standing military relationship.[122] Saudi interest in Pakistan's SSM production was evident as early as 1999, when Prince Sultan visited that country's defense industry. At the time, the Saudi press had reported that he had viewed a film about Pakistan's missiles at the factory where they were produced but that he had not entered the secure areas of the factory.[123] However, the Pakistani nuclear scientist A.Q. Khan more recently has claimed that he had briefed Prince Sultan personally and had shown the latter the actual weaponry, including "the Ghauri missiles [a predecessor to the Shaheen], [and] nuclear weapons (one fitted into a Ghauri warhead)."[124] In early 2014, *Newsweek* reporting, based on an unnamed, "well-placed intelligence source," confirmed that Saudi Arabia had indeed bought the CSS-5 from China in 2007. Ostensibly, the deal occurred with U.S. approval, with American inspectors satisfied that the new missiles "were not designed to carry nukes."[125]

As Lewis suggests, by using such veiled hints, the Saudi government may have wanted to provide a less ambiguous indication to a broader audience—whether Iran, Israel, or the West—of its enhanced arsenal as a way to bolster its deterrent credibility.[126] In addition, of course, Riyadh would thereby reassure domestic audiences about the government's effectiveness in providing for national defense—which remains an important element of legitimacy—as well as regional audiences, since Riyadh sought to expand its influence, particularly in the GCC, where it has promoted itself to sometimes reluctant neighbors as an effective protector. The timing could be explained not only by Iran's continuing threats but also in light of the latter's showcasing of its own SSM capabilities and rumblings of advances in the nuclear field. The Saudi government was probably pleased that there was publicity of this kind spread by foreign sources, thereby enhancing its deterrent. And, Riyadh often permits the local media to report (albeit without commentary) news of such foreign claims, fulfilling a domestic political purpose with plausible denial.[127]

There had already been hints to be gleaned in the Saudi media for a number of years that the country's inventory of SSMs might have been upgraded. According to a 2010 press article based on unnamed military sources, for example, foreign experts from an unspecified Asian country were said to be supervising the missile development program in Saudi Arabia. The report added that Saudi Arabia had been involved in such development activities since 1996. Although the report was originally carried on a Yemeni site, it was reproduced in a Saudi newspaper, *Jazan News*, one whose supervising editor is a Saudi prince, lending some credibility to or at least hinting at the approval of its contents within official circles.[128] This report claimed that Saudi Arabia had purchased the CSS-5 and CSS-6 and was pursuing efforts to upgrade those systems, as well as exploring a possible deal with South Africa for launchers.[129] Likewise, although citing the Scherck book as a source that Saudi Arabia had acquired the CSS-5, in 2011 a Saudi aerospace engineer and head of the Saudi Air and Space Sciences Organization, who writes frequently on defense issues, took that development for granted and argued that Saudi Arabia had a right to do so, although denying that his country had nuclear warheads for the SSMs.[130] Some participants in Saudi discussion fora assumed, at least by 2012, that it was common knowledge that the country now had CSS-5 and CSS-6.[131]

According to reports in a Lebanese newspaper, during discussions in December 2013 between Russian President Vladimir Putin and then-Director of Saudi Intelligence Prince Bandar, at the time in charge of Saudi policy on Syria, the latter had asked for medium range SSMs on behalf of Egypt, with Saudi Arabia and the United Arab Emirates providing the financing. However, Putin was said to have refused, alleging that Riyadh wanted the missiles for Egypt in order to strike at Iran, and noting that medium-range missiles were banned by the treaty signed earlier with the United States.[132] If this report is accurate, Riyadh's intent in having Egypt acquire a ballistic missile system remains unclear. Possibilities include for Riyadh to benefit from the technology transfer, to develop greater strategic depth with an SSM force in a friendly country whose missile bases are less vulnerable to Iranian strikes than those in Saudi Arabia, or even to facilitate a covert transfer of some of the SSMs to Saudi hands.

Is Saudi Arabia able to modify SSMs or warheads domestically, even if only with help from foreign experts? And, if its current inventory of SSMs is not nuclear-capable, in the event the country did go nuclear could that change? The idea of manufacturing SSMs domestically, however unrealistic, is a popular one among Saudi bloggers, as well as in some media and military circles. (See Figure 7)

For example, one student on a Saudi university blog in 2007 found it galling that Iran was able to manufacture its own SSMs "while the Saudis waste their time with camel beauty pageants." In 2006, a Saudi aerospace engineer, stressing the importance of SSMs and ruing the West's restrictions on SSM technology transfer, asked rhetorically "has the Umma understood the lessons and will it begin to prepare to defend itself?"[133] And, the following year, perhaps in an aspirational vein, he called for the Arab states to "enter the age of missile manufacturing."[134] A senior Saudi officer, for his part, stressed the importance of acquiring the technology to manufacture and maintain SSMs, claiming that due to the proliferation of suppliers it is now easy to not only buy such systems, but also to obtain the technologies to either manufacture or modify SSMs, and that it is relatively easy to perform such modifications.[135]

Even if not for manufacturing, it would appear that Saudi Arabia has still been seeking SSM-related technology abroad and that it may have already developed some resident capability—whether thanks to local or foreign experts—to at least modify SSMs. Prince Bandar himself has claimed that the accuracy of Saudi Arabia's SSMs "had since been improved by indigenous modifications."[136] In 2009, significantly, the United States raised questions with Ukraine about a planned transfer of SSM technology to Saudi Arabia, citing the fact that such "category one" SSM technology is suitable to vehicles for delivering WMD, despite assurances by Ukrainian officials that that was not what it would be used for.[137] And, Saudi universities have sent engineering student delegations to visit South Korean factories, including those for the manufacture of space satellites and missiles.[138] In April 2013, Prince Khalid, then still Deputy Minister of Defense, visited China for high-level discussions and toured Poly Group Corporation, a defense conglomerate whose sale of products included the original missile sale to Saudi Arabia.[139] Although the Saudi media did not connect the company with the production of missiles, since photos of his visit to Poly were made public, the intent was probably to send a subtle message to Iran and other foreign governments. (See Figure 8)

And, according to a 2013 blog posting by a former member of the SRF, personnel from the latter go on study tours to Pakistan and China, suggesting continuing cooperation in the missile field with both these countries.

CONSIDERING A NUCLEAR ENVIRONMENT

With its assumed recent modernization, the SRF will play an increasingly important role in the country's defense strategy, especially if Riyadh were to also acquire nuclear weapons. Whatever the conventional impact that Saudi Arabia's SSMs may have, their operational value would increase enormously if paired with nuclear weapons. Saudi spokesmen have suggested, albeit indirectly, on numerous occasions that Riyadh could well follow suit if Iran acquired nuclear weapons, while the country's military and civilian media have done so openly. For example, Prince Muqrin, Saudi Arabia's then-Director General of Saudi Arabia's Intelligence Agency (and now Deputy Crown Prince), already in 2006 had warned indirectly that the proliferation of nuclear weapons in the Middle East, that is to Iran, would "also spur moderate states in the region to establish nuclear programs, whether covertly or openly, aimed at creating a military balance in the region."[140] A more explicit message in this vein was the private communication from King Abd-Allah to U.S. diplomat Dennis Ross in April 2009, when the Saudi monarch told the latter that "If they [i.e. the Iranians] get nuclear weapons, we will get nuclear weapons."[141]

Riyadh has long viewed Israel as a threat to the Arab world, given its imposing SSM and nuclear capabilities, and Tel Aviv's assumed possession of nuclear weapons for decades has led to ingrained Saudi perceptions, at least in public opinion, of a continuing active Israeli nuclear threat, and a future Iranian threat would only join, rather than displace, the existing Israeli one. Thus, one Saudi observer in 2006 typically characterized "the Arabs [as] between the pincers of the Israeli and of the Iranian nuclear deterrents."[142] Such perceptions have persisted and, in 2010, another editorialist spoke of the Arabs as living "between the two halves of a pincer, one of which is Iran … in connection with its nuclear program, and the other of which is Israel."[143] (See Figure 9)

However, over the past few years Riyadh has become increasingly concerned about a more immediate Iranian threat and has viewed Iran's development of SSMs, as was the case in one military journal, within the context of Tehran's perceived intent "to become a regional great power and to be able to impose its hegemony on the region" and in and of themselves as a tool for diplomatic leverage.[144] Similarly, another article in a Saudi military publication, devoted to Iranian SSM advances, pointed out that Iran's focus on SSMs was to "make Iran into the region's great power so as to enable it to impose its hegemony," with the author worrying that Iran's SSM progress would upset the regional balance.[145] In particular, Saudi threat perceptions of Iranian SSMs must be viewed in the context of what the Saudis have assumed is Iran's quest for nuclear weapons, and Saudi pundits often pair Iran's SSM and nuclear programs as a package.[146] Even current developments in Iran's SSM arsenal are viewed in Saudi circles as an indicator of Tehran's intent to acquire nuclear weapons. As one Saudi editorialist put it, "Perhaps it is not far from most people's minds that the missiles that Iran is developing with a capability to reach long distances in space carrying a monkey or other [payloads] are in themselves messages that [Iran] has the capability to deliver its nuclear weapons at long ranges."[147] In that vein, Saudi observers were concerned that although Iran was now willing to negotiate with foreign countries on its nuclear program it was continuing to refuse doing so as far as its SSMs were concerned, at least as of early 2014.[148]

During the last decade, discussions began to appear in the Saudi media as to which country—Israel or Iran—posed the greater threat as a nuclear power and, as a consequence, where the Saudi defense focus should be. As Saudi Arabia increasingly came to believe that Iran was approaching nuclear status, attention began to shift to the latter as a more immediate and in key ways a more pernicious threat. According to one study in a Saudi military journal, what was of particular worry with Iran's acquisition of nuclear weapons was "the difference that in the case of Iran it has become clear that the latter has a geo-political plan for expansion," and that it would now have the ability to establish its hegemony in the region by changing borders, partitioning existing states into mini-states, and turning the Arab states into satellites.[149] Saudi Foreign Minister Prince Saud al-Faysal put the nuclear threat in perspective in 2009, noting that Israel's nuclear arsenal had been a threat for decades already, but if Iran now also acquired nuclear weapons that would "upset the traditional balance between the countries of the Gulf to Iran's favor." As he saw it, "we have every legitimate right to express our legitimate concern and our justified fears of any developments that lead to the proliferation of WMD in the Gulf region … and we also have the right to confirm our categorical refusal of any unilateral hegemony and influence at the expense of our countries, peoples, and interests, or of any plans which transform our countries and peoples into chess pawns."[150]

However low the probability of a nuclear war, some—and perhaps even most—Saudis do not dismiss it offhand, not excluding the possibility that Iran might use a nuclear capability in a warfighting mode. Thus, one commentator in a Saudi-owned newspaper was critical of those who felt that Iran would not use nuclear weapons against an Arab state, given that it was Muslim, by pointing out that Iran had already used chemical weapons in the Iran-Iraq War against Iraq.[151] Another editorial in 2013 was skeptical that deterrence could work with Iran, claiming that the Iranian leadership was unpredictable, and that even potential alternatives to the current leaders believed in the return of the awaited Mahdi and might be willing to hasten the process at any cost. The editorial concluded by asking "How, then, can we trust a nuclear Iran?"[152] Likewise, some Saudis believed that Israel "would not hesitate to use whatever WMD it had, including nuclear weapons, in any future war with the Arabs" not only as a last resort but even in other situations, such as not being able to deal with a conventional Arab attack.[153]

Almost universally, what stands out in Saudi discussions within policy, military, and civilian circles is the consensus around the belief of the validity and effectiveness of nuclear deterrence. In drawing lessons learned from the past, the Saudis repeatedly refer not only to the relationships between the United States and the Soviet Union during the Cold War, but also to Pakistan and India, and North Korea and the United States as proof that mutual nuclear deterrence is an effective mechanism to ensure security and stability.[154] In fact, Saudi analysts—and no doubt policymakers—believe that this "strategic stability" based on nuclear weapons continues to this day as the basis of the security relationship between the United States and Russia, and the difficulty in reducing the number of nuclear arms "shows the extent to which states are [still] focused on that."[155] As a senior military officer expressed it, "Contemporary states began to realize clearly that their existence and their ability to protect their populations against any foreign aggression is tied intimately with its national security which, in turn, will not be achieved except by developing defensive weapons, uppermost of which are nuclear weapons, which support deterrence against foreign aggressors."[156]

The perceived need for the consolidation of a credible Saudi deterrent and a potential warfighting capability increased in parallel with Riyadh's concern about Iran, particularly in view of the uncertainties about the reliability of American guarantees, with questions about the depth of Washington's commitment to support its allies in the region. Revealingly, senior Saudi policy-makers were reportedly upset by what they interpreted to have been the United States' abrupt abandonment of its close regional ally, Egyptian President Hosni Mubarak, which raised doubts in their minds about the reliability in other cases of expected U.S. support and protection. Prince Turki al-Faysal, for example, probably reflecting impressions at the senior levels of the royal family, remarked on the irritation with "the haste with which the American leadership … pushed President Hosni Mubarak out of power, even before the Egyptian people had expressed their opinion … this angered me personally … Saudi citizens [on the contrary] are faithful to their friends and allies ... if only [President Barack Obama] had waited a little and let the Egyptian people make their own decision."[157] This malaise was reinforced more recently by the Saudi discomfort with the rapprochement between the United States and Iran. In fact, many in the tightly-controlled Saudi media began to worry openly that a U.S.-Iranian rapprochement could mean a basic change in American policy in the Middle East, with Washington seeing in Iran its partner of choice rather than the Arabs. Saudi opinionmakers also feared a secret U.S.-Iranian deal was approaching, with Washington recognizing Iran as a nuclear power and acknowledging its traditional role as the "Gulf policeman," that is the hegemonic power in the Gulf, in order to balance Saudi Arabia and Turkey.[158] The Saudi media expressed concern all along that it would be "the Arabs" or "the Gulf" who could pay the price of a possible U.S.-Iranian deal.[159] And, accompanying the Saudis' perception of U.S. weakness on Syria, some in the Saudi media interpreted U.S. policy on the Russia-Ukraine 2014 confrontation as further evidence.[160] Of course, this did not mean that the U.S.-Saudi relationship was in danger of ending anytime soon. In effect, in late October 2013, the political editor of the country's leading daily, *Al-Riyadh*, reminded readers that although the U.S.-Saudi bilateral relationship was "vulnerable to shocks" nevertheless "no one expects the relationship to collapse," given the robust economic, security, and political interests that bind the two countries together.[161] What such trends did indicate, however, was that Riyadh would likely follow a more independent policy, as the country's ambassador to Great Britain suggested.[162] In defense matters, in line with this sense to rely on one's self as much as possible, when referring to a potential Iranian nuclear threat, one Saudi observer likewise noted that "the West cannot always be relied upon, and those in the Gulf are the ones best suited to defend their own security."[163]

SSMs will play a significant part in Riyadh's deterrence policy, even as conventional weapons. As a senior Saudi Air Defense Force officer noted, one of the key reasons why states seek SSMs—and one can assume that although not stated the same considerations also apply to Saudi Arabia in his view—is that "Missiles in all their forms are among the most lethal forms of mass destruction that modern technology has generated in the military sphere."[164] What is also significant is that some Saudis have made an open argument linking SSMs and WMD in their advocacy. For example, an editorial by a Saudi political scientist who has served as an adviser on his country's National Security Council, not only called on "the Arabs" (a term often used as a veiled allusion to Saudi Arabia) to acquire nuclear weapons but also added that "Having nuclear weapons is meaningless in strategic terms as long as there is not a parallel development of a delivery system for such weapons to reach the intended targets."[165] In fact, Saudi military writers often explicitly present SSMs, nuclear weapons, and space-based capabilities as a cohesive package. As a senior Saudi officer put it, "All studies focused on the proliferation of a strategic capability—in its three facets of missile, space, and nuclear—indicate that all countries have numerous motivations ... I consider the most important motivation to be the quest for status which will give a state regional and international influence ... in relation to the countries in its region."[166] One can also expect an improvement in the SSMs' capabilities if there is further development in the space sector, as the same senior Saudi officer emphasized the significance of having a space-based capability in relation to SSMs, linking space-based early warning, command and control, and targeting with SSMs.[167]

THE APRIL 2014 SWORD OF ABD-ALLAH EXERCISE: CONNECTING THE DOTS

The two-week-long April 2014 Sword of Abd-Allah Exercise was a landmark event for Saudi Arabia's SRF and for the country's military in general. This exercise represented the largest such maneuvers ever held in the country and was a joint effort, including all the military services, the National Guard, and the Ministry of the Interior, and took place in three separate theaters. Specifically for the SRF, this exercise also represented the first time that the actual SSMs went on public display, as two missiles were included in the final ceremonial parade. Only the CSS-2 missiles, acquired in the 1980s, were put on display, and the Saudis went out of their way to ensure that even non-expert audiences understood that that was the missile system being shown by painting DF-3 (the Chinese model number for the CSS-2) on the side of the missiles, as appeared in some of the official media photos. Elsewhere, the Saudi press reported that the RSF had participated in the operational exercise, although it was not specified in what capacity that had occurred.[168] (See Figure 10)

In many ways, the public display of the missiles and the accompanying Saudi commentary did much to crystallize and underline the broader enduring themes of Riyadh's thinking, such as its mistrust of Iranian policy and conviction that Tehran intends to continue its quest to acquire nuclear weapons despite any agreements reached, unease about the reliability of U.S. security guarantees, pique at some of the GCC states for their more benign outlook on Iran, national pride, faith in the effectiveness of the concept of deterrence, the portrayal of nuclear weapons and SSM as a package, and a renewed warning of the Saudi option to pursue a nuclear deterrent if Iran does so.

The Saudi government no doubt intended to use this occasion, in particular, as a mechanism in support of both its defense strategy and of wider-ranging policy aims. The SSMs were paraded prominently for the attending foreign dignitaries, as well as highlighted in Saudi newspapers and on TV. The accompanying media accounts were standardized and followed the still limited official narrative, although follow-on commentary elaborated for domestic, regional and international audiences on the importance of the exercise.

Unofficial spokesmen noted openly that the Saudi government wanted to send political messages to several different audiences with the exercise and by publicizing its SSMs. As one editorial stressed, Riyadh's "strategic missiles were of overriding importance as an indicator" of its message.[169] As if to ensure that the intended parties understood the message, one commentator underlined that Saudi Arabia is not one to make empty boasts or to engage in military propaganda, and that Riyadh really did want to "send clear messages to several intended parties."[170] Perhaps uppermost, as one commentator noted, was "a message specifically for [Saudi Arabia's] Iranian neighbor, who seeks to acquire nuclear weapons."[171] The same commentator saw the CSS-2, in particular, as "a message to those forces that harbor evil intent for the security of Saudi Arabia and the Gulf." Elsewhere, the same journalist, again citing specifically the CSS-2, warned that Saudi Arabia had shown that "it can cut off any hand raised against it" and quipped that even though the Iranians were not present at the exercise, Oman would probably pass on the message to Tehran, a not too subtle jab at Oman for its good relations with the latter.[172] In addition, many pundits in the Saudi media pointed out that there was also a message of warning to Saudi Arabia's other neighbors, including Israel, Syria, and Iraq.

As part of the same message, the Saudi media now also revived a recurring theme, namely that Saudi Arabia could provide an effective security umbrella for its neighbors. According to one commentator, with the Sword of Abd-Allah Exercise, "Saudi Arabia has become a different country, one that has military deterrent power for all, and not just for its immediate neighbors," and, moreover, "everyone has understood the message that the Kingdom is capable of defending its own holy lands as well as its allies in the region."[173] Another journalist, likewise, concluded that the exercise was intended to show that Saudi Arabia "has the ability to slap down any transgressor who thinks he can violate the security and stability of our country and of the brotherly Gulf countries."[174] Some wanted to reiterate that the Exercise was an expression of disappointment with, and a message to, the United States, which one commentator accused of not only still being hesitant in dealing decisively with Iran, but also of not being quick in understanding a message.[175] As part of this message, other Saudi observers also claimed that the exercise provided proof of Riyadh's self-reliance, and that Saudi Arabia "does not need anyone to defend it as the western and the hostile media maintain."[176]

The Sword of Abd-Allah Exercise also highlighted the importance of the domestic audience in securing the Saudi royal family's legitimacy. As one Saudi editorial noted, "the first message of the Sword of [Abd-] Allah [Exercise] was to reassure the homeland on the readiness of our armed forces."[177] According to another Saudi observer, "the Saudi public was also included in the exercise's message, since mobilization is one of the most important aspects of [national] discipline."[178] Not surprisingly, Saudi press commentaries portrayed the CSS-2 as a source of national pride and saw the missiles as a significant achievement for the government. For example, one journalist reported that the appearance of the CSS-2 was accompanied by "enthusiastic applause by his highness [Minister of Defense Prince Salman] and by the audience."[179] The same commentator claimed elsewhere that learning about the CSS-2 had engendered "an enthusiastic response from the Saudi public."[180] In the wake of the exercise, one editorialist, citing the power that had been displayed, linked that to national security and, in turn, to "a leadership that has wisdom and is willing to listen to all opinions ... and who will introduce anything new in order to support its determination."[181]

In addition, some in the media hinted obliquely that Saudi Arabia might have assets beyond the CSS-2. One commentator, for example, warned after the exercise that "the East Wind [i.e. CSS-2 missiles] were only the beginning of what Saudi policy conduct may be in the future."[182] Another Saudi editorialist noted that Riyadh "revealed only a small part of the advanced military systems in its possession."[183] More broadly, this same commentator also alluded to the relationship between SSMs and nuclear weapons, albeit indirectly. Alleging that Iran trumpets its own SSMs and its assumed nuclear weapons program in the media for propaganda purposes, he countered that "nuclear weapons are not such a big deal," specifically because "many Islamic countries have [also] acquired that ... The Kingdom, however, does not need to always say things openly and to respond to the Iranian farces by telling what it has."[184]

Significantly, an additional message was directed more openly to the local audience using local electronic newspapers, as these media outlets have a local readership and are not likely to attract international attention. Perhaps assuming that international audiences would make the appropriate deductions anyhow and wanting to ensure that domestic readers did not miss a key element, the specific point was almost invariably raised in the local media, using standardized language, to the effect that the CSS-2 displayed during the Sword of Abd-Allah Exercise "is capable of carrying nuclear warheads."[185] That is, tying the SSMs to a potential nuclear capability may have been intended to convince local and regional audiences that the country's leadership is providing adequately for defense and is prepared to meet any potential threat, including a nuclear one. One Saudi electronic newspaper was particularly explicit with its hints on this score. Citing the CSS-2, this source underscored the "the nuclear dimension" of the message, thus openly hinting at a linkage between the SSMs and a nuclear capability. And, this observer went on to stress that the CSS-2 was not only nuclear-capable but that in the audience watching the parade was the chief of staff of "nuclear Pakistan" and suggested there was now a new alliance with "nuclear Pakistan."[186] Likewise, the Saudi edition of the *Al-Hayat* international Arabic-language daily, which the royal family owns, also suggested that the CSS-2 shown was not the only SSM in the national arsenal, as it spoke openly of the Saudis as having "the East Wind missiles and other strategic missiles."[187]

In the days following the parade, the Saudi media basked in the reaction of the Israeli and Iranian media to seeing the SSMs, which the Saudi media interpreted as surprise and alarm in those countries' official circles. The standardized accounts of such reactions, as carried in the Saudi media, suggested an official effort, probably intended to further boost the government's credibility with the local audience. However, an unintended consequence may be the strengthening of the hardliners' hand in Tehran on the nuclear issue and on its own SSMs.

CONCLUSIONS

Several conclusions may be drawn from the preceding study.

First, Saudi Arabia considers its SSMs as a key component of its force structure and will continue to do so. In light of its threat assessment, its growing mistrust of international guarantees, and desire to display its independence, Riyadh can be expected to continue devoting significant assets to the SRF and to work to improve the latter's material and human capabilities.

Second, the primary focus of Saudi Arabia's SRF will continue to be on deterrence. However, given the fine line between deterrence and warfighting, and based on past experience, if the situation became sufficiently grave, Riyadh would be willing to employ its missiles in a warfighting mode as well, and perhaps even preemptively.

Third, the apparent recent upgrade in the SSM force, if confirmed, is an additional indication that Saudi Arabia is likely to consider following suit if Iran succeeds in developing a nuclear capability—almost assuredly by direct acquisition of a ready-made capability from abroad, and very likely from Pakistan—especially given the Saudi view of SSM and nuclear weapons as an interrelated package. To some extent, Riyadh presumably sees an SSM capability as part of its deterrent effort designed to convince Iran not to pursue nuclear weapons by lending credibility to its threats to also acquire and be able to deliver nuclear weapons if Iran were to do so. Even if the on-going negotiations with Iran lead to a permanent agreement by which Tehran would forswear pursuing nuclear weapons, Riyadh would likely still retain and develop its missile capabilities as a reserve to respond in case of any Iranian nuclear breakout in the future.

Fourth, one can interpret the timing of the display of the SSMs, just after the visits by President Barack Obama to Saudi Arabia in late March 2014 and U.S. Secretary of State John Kerry in April 2014, as Riyadh's continuing lack of complete confidence in U.S. guarantees on Iran.

Fifth, the case of Saudi Arabia suggests that in some instances the international community's leverage to prevent proliferation may be very limited. Admittedly, Saudi Arabia may be a special case, due to its unique position as an international oil powerhouse. However, other countries as well, whether thanks to political or economic advantages, may also be able to resist outside pressure or avert it altogether when they judge that their vital national security interests are at stake.

Sixth, although Saudi Arabia intends its SSMs to have a stabilizing effect in the region by deterring potential aggression and adventurism, such upgraded arsenals also open the way for further arms races and increased regional tensions. As one would imagine, both Israel and Iran have raised concerns about Saudi Arabia's developing SSM arsenal, whether for security or political reasons. However, some in Russia, too, have expressed their unease, however unfounded that may be, about a potential threat to their own country from the Saudi SSMs at some time in the future. According to one analyst, "Of course, today no one in Saudi Arabia is considering attacking Russia. These are not crazy people. But what if radical Islamists of the likes of Osama Bin Laden should come to power there? That would be a gloomy prospect."[188] Furthermore, enhanced capabilities can also contribute to escalation and have the potential for miscalculation in a regional crisis, which would be especially risky if Iran and Saudi Arabia did eventually decide to acquire nuclear weapons.

Finally, counterproliferation efforts in general by the international community on the control of missile technology from potential suppliers as well as recipients, especially given the role of SSMs as the delivery method of choice for emerging nuclear programs, must continue in order to promote genuine stability and to reduce the risk of unintended consequences.

Notes:

[1] On this issue, see Norman Cigar, *Considering a Nuclear Gulf: Thinking about Nuclear Weapons in Saudi Arabia* (Maxwell AFB, Alabama: USAF Counterproliferation Center, November 2013), http://cpc.au.af.mil/pdfs/books/nucleargulf.pdf.

[2] "Waliy al-ahd ya'mur bi-sarf ilawat 25 fi al-mi'a li-mukhtalif qitaat al-quwwat al-musallaha" [The Crown Prince Orders a 25 Per Cent Raise for All the Services of the Armed Forces], *Al-Marsad* (Saudi Arabia), 8 January 2014, http://al-marsd.com.

[3] Prince Khalid bin Sultan quoted in Mansur al-Shihri, "Shahad anshitat tamrin itirad al-sawarikh al-balistiya Khalid bin Sultan" [Khalid bin Sultan Witnessed Exercise Activities Related to Countering Ballistic Missiles], *Ukaz* (Jeddah), 4 November 2009, www.okaz.com.sa/new/Issues/20091104/PrinCon20091104313466.htm.

[4] Interview with Prince Sultan, "Al-Alam al-arabi yamurr bi-marhala harija" [The Arab World Is Going through a Sensitive Period], *Al-Hawadith* (Beirut), 27 April 1990, 18. (hereafter Prince Sultan, "Al-Alam al-arabi")

[5] The intercepted conversation is one of the Iraqi documents captured in 2003, transcript in SH-MICN-D-000-839_TF, 28 July 1990, Conflict Records Research Center, Washington, DC.

[6] HRH General Khaled Bin Sultan, *Desert Warrior* (London: Harper Collins, 1995), 144. (hereafter Prince Khaled, *Desert Warrior*)

[7] Interview with King Fahd, "Khadim al-haramayn yaltaqi bi-mansubi wa-talabat far jamiat Al-Imam Saud al-islamiya bi'l-Qasim" [The Servant of the Two Holy Shrines Meets with the Staff and Students of the Branch of the Imam Saud Islamic University in Al-Qasim], *Ukaz* (Jeddah), 9 April 1988, 7. (hereafter King Fahd, "Khadim al-haramayn")

[8] Interview with Staff Major General Sulayman al-Shayi (Retired) by Rashid al-Sakran, "Lam uqaddim li'l-faqid Sultan mashruan fih maslaha li'l-watan wa-abna'ih fa-rafadhu" [The Late Sultan Did Not Reject Any Project That I Presented to Him That Was of Benefit to This Country and Its Citizens], *Al-Riyadh*, 28 October 2011, www.al-riyadh.com/2011/10/28/article679312.html. (hereafter Al-Shayi, "Lam uqaddim")

[9] Quoted in "Mustaiddun li-muwajahat ayy tari' lan nasmah bi-ayy tadakhkhul fi shu'unna" [We Are Prepared to Confront Any Contingency and We Will Not Permit Any Interference in Our Affairs], *Ukaz*, 29 March 1988, 3.

[10] Prince Khaled, *Desert Warrior*, 145.

[11] Interview with Major General Anwar al-Ashqi (Retired) by Muhammad al-Hilali, "Kayf yuidd Sultan ra'is al-arkan? Wa-ma radduh ala wazir difa Amrika?" [How Did Sultan Prepare the Chief of Staff? What Was His Reply to the U.S. Secretary of Defense?], *Al-Iqtisadiya*, 25 October 2011, www.aleqt.com/2011/1025/article_592734.pda.

[12] Staff Brigadier Zayid bin Muhammad al-Umari, "Dawafi imtilak al-qudrat al-istratijiya al-sarukhiya al-fada'iya wa'l-nawawiya" [The Incentives for Acquiring Strategic Rocket, Space, and Nuclear Capabilities], *Quwwat Al-Difa Al-Jawwi Al-Malaki Al-Saudi*, December 2010, 13. This is the Saudi Air Defense's professional journal. (hereafter Al-Umari, "Dawafi imtilak al-qudrat")

[13] Fawwaz Hamad al-Fawwaz, "Alamat fi al-amn al-watani" [The Characteristics of National Security], *Al-Iqtisadiya* (Jeddah), 21 November 2011, www.aleqt.com/2006/11/21/article_7059.print.

[14] Muhammad Izzat Muhammad Ali, "Al-Sawarikh al-balistiya ard/ard" [Surface-to-surface Ballistic Missiles], *Majallat Kulliyat Al-Malik Khalid Al-Askariya* (Riyadh), 1 September 2008, www.kkmaq.gov/detail.aso?InNewItemID=283786&In TemplateKey=print. This is the Saudi National Guard academy's professional journal. (hereafter Muhammad Ali, "Al-Sawarikh al-balistiya")

[15] Muhammad Rida Nasr Allah, "Malmahan fi siratih" [Two Glimpses of His Life], *Al-Riyadh*, 13 November 2001, www.alriyadh.com/2001/11/13/article30535.html.

[16] Prince Sultan, "Al-Alam al-arabi," 18.

[17] King Fahd, "Khadim al-haramayn," 7.

[18] Interview with King Fahd by Ahmad al-Jar Allah. "Al-Fahd: Anayt ka-ma law ann al-ta'ira al-makhtufa saudiya" [Fahd: I Suffered As If the Hijacked Airplane Were a Saudi One], *Al-Siyasa* (Kuwait), 28-29 April 1988, 7.

[19] King Abd-Allah reported in Umar al-Zubaydi, "Bakin wa'l-Riyadh aqdan min al-alaqat al-saudiya al-siniya bawwabatha al-iqtisad" [Beijing and Riyadh: Two Decades of Saudi-Chinese Relations Whose Gateway Is the Economy], *Al-Watan* (Abha, Saudi Arabia), 21 September 2010, www.alwatan.com.sa/Dialogue/News_Detail.aspx?ArticleID=21892&CategoryID=4.

[20] Jim Mann, "U.S. Caught Napping by Sino-Saudi Missile Deal," *Los Angeles Times*, 4 May 1988, 1.

[21] Prince Bandar quoted in William Simpson, *The Prince: The Secret Story of the World's Most Intriguing Royal, Prince Bandar Bin Sultan* (New York: Regan, 2006), 156. This work is a semi-official biography based largely on interviews with Prince Bandar. (hereafter Simpson, *The Prince*)

[22] Prince Khaled, *Desert Warrior*, 150.

[23] Quoted in Simpson, *The Prince*, 162.

[24] Prince Khaled, *Desert Warrior*, 151.

[25] Prince Faysal quoted in "Rakab sayyarat Datsun li-ziyarat marid" [He Rode in A Datsun Car to Go Visit a Sick Man], *Sabq* (Riyadh), 24 October 2011, http://sabq.org/sabq/user/news.do?id=32236&section=5&print=true.

[26] King Fahd, "Khadim al-haramayn," 7.

[27] "Hasalna ala sawarikh mutafawwiqa li'l-difa an muqaddasatna" [We Acquired Advanced Missiles in Order to Defend Our Holy Places], *Ukaz*, 20 March 1988, 1.

[28] Prince Sultan, "Al-Alam al-arabi," 19.

[29] Quoted in Simpson, *The Prince*, 156.

[30] Interview with Prince Sultan, "Al-Amir Sultan: Ishtarayna al-sawarikh min Al-Sin li-annaha dawla muhayida bayn al-imlaqayn" [Prince Sultan: We Bought the Missiles from China Because It Is a Neutral Country between the Two Giants], *Al-Sayyad* (Beirut), 29 April 1988, 35. (hereafter Prince Sultan, "Al-Amir Sultan")

[31] Reported in Turki al-Suhayyil, "Al-Saudiya: Al-Amir Khalid bin Sultan yaftatih mansha'at al-sawarikh al-istratijiya" [Saudi Arabia: Prince Khalid bin Sultan Inaugurates a Strategic Rocket Facility], *Al-Sharq Al-Awsat* (London), 3 March 2010, www.aawsat.com/print.asp?did=559516&issueno=11418. (hereafter Al-Suhayyil, "Al-Saudiya")

[32] "Al-Qiyada wa'l-qitaat al-askariya" [The Leadership and the Military Sectors], *Al-Jazira* (Riyadh), 5 December 1999, www.al-jazirah.com/1999/19991205/ln10.htm. (hereafter "Al-Qiyada wa'l-qitaat")

[33] Al-Suhayyil, "Al-Saudiya."

[34] Ibid.

[35] Ibid.

[36] "Al-Qiyada wa'l-qitaat."

[37] King Saud University website, www.cksu.com/vb/forum.php.

[38] A'id Al-Qarni, "Al-Gharb yujahid wa-yuharrim alayna al-jihad" [The West Carries on a Jihad But Prohibits Us from Doing So], *Al-Sharq Al-Awsat*, 8 November 2011, www.aawsat.com/print.asp?did=648856&issueno=12033.

[39] Ibid.

[40] [Major General] Yusuf bin Ibrahim al-Sallum (Retired), "Ru'ya istratijiya mustaqbaliya" [A Future Strategic Vision], *Al-Jazira*, 11 October 2005, www.al-jazirah.com/2005/20051011/rj2.htm.

[41] Staff Brigadier General Muhammad bin Yahya al-Jadii, "Idad al-istiratijiya al-askariya: al-tahaddiyat wa'l-suubat" [Preparing Military Strategy: The Challenges and the Difficulties], *Quwwat Al-Difa Al-Jawwi Al-Malaki Al-Saudi* (Riyadh), 13 December 2011, www.rsadf.gov.sa/Pub_mq1T.asp?ID=6.

[42] Ibid.

[43] Prince Khaled, *Desert Warrior*, 145, 149.

[44] Al-Umari, "Dawafi imtilak al-qudrat," 13.

[45] Reported in Al-Suhayyil, "Al-Saudiya."

[46] Quoted in Simpson, *The Prince*, 156; also, Prince Khaled, *Desert Warrior*, 150.

[47] Quoted in Simpson, *The Prince*, 156.

[48] Prince Khaled, *Desert Warrior*, 150.

[49] Quoted in Simpson, *The Prince*, 158.

[50] "Reprimand Urged for Shamir Aide Who Leaked News about Saudi Missiles," *Jewish Telegraphic Agency* (Jerusalem), 21 March 1988, www.jta.org.

[51] George C. Wilson and David B. Ottoway, "Saudi-Israeli Tensions Worry U.S.; Bombing Practice May Presage Attack on Missiles in Arabia," *Washington Post*, 25 March 1988. A1.

[52] Quoted in "Mustaiddun li-muwajahat ayy tari' lan nasmah bi-ayy tadakhkhul fi shu'unna" [We Are Prepared to Confront Any Contingency and We Will Not Permit Any Interference in Our Affairs], *Ukaz*, 29 March 1988, 3.

[53] Editorial, "Bi-Kull al-quwwa difaan an al-watan wa'l-muqaddasat" [With All Our Power in Defense of the Country and the Holy Places], *Ukaz*, 29 March 1988, 5.

[54] King Fahd, "Khadim al-haramayn," 7.

[55] Prince Sultan, "Al-Amir Sultan," 33.

[56] Quoted in Simpson, *The Prince*, 163.

[57] Ibid, 162.

[58] John H. Cushman Jr., "Reagan Urges Israeli Restraint on Saudi Missiles," *New York Times*, 26 March 1988, www.nytimes.com.

[59] Interview with King Fahd by Ahmad al-Jar Allah. "Al-Fahd: Anayt ka-ma law ann al-ta'ira al-makhtufa saudiya" [Fahd: I Suffered As If the Hijacked Airplane Was a Saudi One], *Al-Siyasa* (Kuwait), 28-29 April 1988, 7.

[60] "Report: China Selling Saudi Arabia Intermediate–Range Missiles," *Associated Press*, 17 March 1988, www.apnewsarchive.com.

[61] "Saudi CSS-2 Missiles Now Operational," *Flight International* (London), 6-12 June 1990, 12-13.

[62] Al-Asali, "Al-Tahaddiyat al-iraniya."

[63] Ibid.

[64] Prince Khaled, *Desert Warrior*, 145.

[65] Speech by Prince Sultan, "Al-Amir Sultan: Quwwatna mutakamilat al-taslih wa-qadirun ala al-hasm al-sari wa-namlik sawarikh qadira ala al-tadmir" [Prince Sultan: Our Forces Are Fully Armed and We Are Able to Decide Quickly and We Possess Missiles That Can Destroy], *Al-Riyadh*, 5 September 1990, 1, 9.

[66] Press conference with Prince Khalid, "Al-Amir al-fariq awwal rukn Khalid bin Sultan qa'id al-difa al-jawwi wa'l-quwwat al-mushtaraka" [Staff Lieutenant General Prince Khalid bin Sultan Commander of the Air Defense and of the Combined Forces], *Al-Riyadh*, 28 August 1990, 5.

[67] Prince Khalid bin Sultan, "Hiwar sari ma qa'id al-quwwat al-mushtaraka fi harb Al-Khalij" [A Quick Interview with the Commander of the Combined Forces during the Gulf War], *Al-Ahram* (Cairo), 28 February 1992, 5. (hereafter Prince Khalid, "Hiwar sari")

[68] Ibid.

[69] Ibid.

[70] Ibid.

[71] "Rudud al-afal al-iqlimiya wa'l-alamiya li'l-darabat al-sarukhiya" [The Regional and International Responses to the Missile Strikes], Prince Khalid bin Sultan's website, www.moqatel.com/openshare/Behoth/IraqKwit24/sec06.doc_cvt.htm. (hereafter Prince Khalid, "Rudud al-afal")

[72] Ibid.

[73] Prince Khalid, "Hiwar sari."

[74] Prince Khalid, "Rudud al-afal."

[75] Prince Khalid, "Hiwar sari."

[76] Interview by Aleksandr Popov, "Rossiiskie strategicheskie bombardirovshchiki pod bokom u korolei i presidentov" [Strategic Russian Bombers Are Quite Near to the Kings and Presidents], *Telegrafist* (Moscow), 4 July 2013, reproduced on Maxpark website (Moscow), http://maxpark.com/community/832/content/2070974.

[77] For example, "Tawattur siyasi ghayr masbuq bayn Al-Saudiya wa-Rusiya wa-tahdidat bi-qasf Al-Riyadh" [Unprecedented Tension between Saudi Arabia and Russia and Threats to Bomb Riyadh], *Sabq*, 28 June 2014, http://sabq.org/ky7fde, and "Mawqi rusi: Rusiya tukhattit li-darb Al-Riyadh wa'l-Dawha abr al-ajwa' al-iraniya" [A Russian Website: Russia Is Planning to Strike Riyadh and Doha through Iranian Airspace], *Al-Marsad* (Riyadh), 29 June 2014, http://al-marsd.com/c-74280.

[78] For example, "Suhaf: Rusiya tuhaddid bi-qasf Al-Riyadh" [The Press: Russia Threatens to Bomb Riyadh], CNNArabic.com, 30 June 2014, http://archive.cnn.com/2013/middle_east/6/29/Apprs.sat29jun, and "Mawqi rusi: Tawattur siyasi bayn Al-Mamlaka wa-Rusiya wa-tahdidat bi-qasf l-Riyadh wa'l-Dawha abr al-ajwa' al-iraniya" [Russian Website: Political Tension between the Kingdom and Russia and Threats to Bomb Riyadh and Doha through Iranian Airspace], MSN Arabia,29 June 2014, http://arabic.arabia.msn.com.

[79] For example, the Unayza and Utayba tribal websites, www.onaizatoday.com/news .php?action=show&id=4495, and www.otaibah.net/m/showthread.php?t=144720.

[80] "Saudiyun raddan ala tahdidat Rusiya bi-qasf Al-Riyadh" [Saudis Respond to Russia's Threats to Bomb Riyadh], *Qabas* (Riyadh), 12 August 2014, http://qbas.org/home/news-action-show-id-6742.htm.

[81] Ahmad Baashan, "Saffarat indhar marra ukhra!" [Alarm Sirens Once Again!], *Sabq*, 9 February 2014, http://sabq.org/dx1aCd.

[82] Staff Major General Jar Allah al-Alwit, "Al-Amir Salman yazur qiyadatay al-quwwat al-jawwiya wa'l-sawarikh al-istratijiya" [Prince Salman Visits the Headquarters of the Air Force and of the SRF], *Al-Riyadh*, 27 November 2011, www.alriyadh.com/2011/11/27/article686327.html. (hereafter Al-Alwit, "Al-Amir Salman yazur")

[83] Muhammad Ali, "Al-Sawarikh al-balistiya."

[84] [Lieutenant General] Wafiq al-Samarra'i, "Al-Tasalluh al-irani wa-kayfiyat mualajatih" [Iran's Arming and How to Deal with It], *Al-Sharq Al-Awsat*, 7 March 2009, www.aawsat.com/leader.asp?section=3&issueno=11057&Article=509970.

[85] Abd-Allah bin Fahd al-Luhaydan, "Al-Difa al-istratiji wa'l-nizham al-duwali" [Strategic Defense and the World Order], *Al-Jazira*,7 July 2000, www.al-jazirah.com/2000/20000707/ar2.htm.

[86] "Sumuw na'ib wazir al-difa raa hafl iftitah buhayrat muntazah Al-Amir Abd al-Rahman al-tarfihi bi-Wadi Al-

Dawasir" [His Highness the Deputy Defense Minister Presides over the Inauguration Ceremonies for the Lakes of Prince Abd al-Rahman Recreational Park in Wadi Al-Dawasir], *Al-Jazira*, 17 June 2000, www.al-jazirah.com/2000/20000617/t/ln4.htm. (hereafter "Sumuw na'ib wazir al-difa")

[87] Qablan al-Hazimi, "Al-Amir Abd al-Rahman raa half takhrij adad min al-dawrat bi-markaz quwwat al-sawarikh al-istratijiya bi-Wadi Al-Dawasir" [Prince Abd al-Rahman Presides over the Graduation Ceremony of Several Courses at the SRF Center], *Al-Jazira*, 29 June 2005, www.al-jazirah.com/2005/20050629/ln5t.htm. (hereafter Al-Hazimi, "Al-Amir Abd al-Rahman")

[88] "Musaid wazir al-difa wa'l-tayaran yara al-tamrin al-tabawi li-itirad sawarikh al-batriyut li'l-sawarikh al-balis-tiya" [The Deputy Minister of Defense and Air Presides over the Operational Exercise of the Patriot Countering Ballistic Missiles], *Ayn Al-Yaqin* (Saudi Arabia), 6 November 2009, www.aynalyaqeen.comarch_2009/6-nov/ar2.php.

[89] Abd al-Jalil Zayd al-Marhun, "Amn al-Khalij … hal min mutaghayyir amiriki jadid?" [Gulf Security… Is There a New American Shift?], *Al-Riyadh*, 20 March 2009, www.alriyadh.com/2009/03/20/article417096.html.

[90] Muhammad Ali, "Al-Sawarikh al-balistiya."

[91] Awad Mani al-Qahtani, "Uqb riaayatih faaliyat tamrin itlaq al-sawarikh al-itiradiya al-balistiya" [After He Presided over the Exercise Activities of the Launch of the Anti-Ballistic-Missile Missiles], *Al-Jazira*, 4 November 2009, www.al-jazirah.com.sa/2009jaz/nov/4/fe15.htm.

[92] "Sumuw al-amir Sultan yaud ila Al-Riyadh ams" [His Highness Prince Sultan Returned to Riyadh Yesterday], *Al-Madina* (Jeddah), 1 March 1992, 11. (hereafter "Sumuw al-amir Sultan")

[93] "Al-Amir Khalid bin Sultan: Al-Qada al-uqala' fi mintaqatna yasaun li-tajannub huduth muwajahat wa-fi al-mam-laka rijal yasharun ala himayatha" [Prince Khalid bin Sultan: The Wise Leaders in Our Region Seek to Avoid Confrontations and in the Kingdom There Are Men Who Lie Awake in Order to Defend It], *Al-Riyadh*, 12 June 2007, www.al-riyadh.com/2007/06/12/article256612.html.

[94] A'id al-Shashai, "Quwwat al-sawarikh yatanafas ala ja'izat hifzh al-qur'an li'l-askariyin" [The Rocket Force Competes for the Prize in the Military's Qur'an Memorization Tournament], *Al-Sharq* (Dammam), 20 February 2012, www.alasharq.net.sa/2012/02/02/108552; and "Afrad min quwwat al-sawarikh bi-Wadi Al-Dawasir yuhaqqiqun al-marakiz al-ula" [Members of the SRF in Wadi Al-Dawasir Achieve First Place], *Arkan* (Saudi Arabia), 28 February 2010, www.arkan-news.com/news.php?action=print&m=&id=1340.

[95] Al-Alwit, "Al-Amir Salman yazur."

[96] Al-Shayi, "Lam uqaddim."

[97] Ibid.

[98] For example, the Commander of the SRF School and Training Center, "Al-Amir Abd Al-Rahman yaftatih mabna tadrib markaz wa-madrasat quwwat al-sawarikh al-istratijiya" [Prince Abd al-Rahman Inaugurates the Training Facility of the SRF Center and School], *Al-Madina*, 11 July 2011, ww.al-madina.com/node/314716.

[99] "Sumuw al-amir Sultan," 11.

[100] "Sumuw waliy al-ahd yaftatih al-mansha'a al-taktikiya wa'l-madina al-sakniya li-qaidat al-sawarikh al-istratijia 511 bi'l-Hariq" [His Highness the Crown Prince Inaugurates the Tactical Facility and the Residential Complex at the Strategic Rocket Base 511 in Al-Hariq], *Al-Jazira*, 5 December 1999, www.al-jazirah.com/1999/19991205/fr1.htm.

[101] "Al-Amir Abd-Allah yatafaqqad qaidat sawarikh istratijiya wast Al-Saudiya" [Prince Abd-Allah Inspects a Strategic Rocket Base in Central Saudi Arabia], Kuwait News Agency, 4 December 1999, www.kuna.net.kw.

[102] "Na'ib wazir al-difa raa takhrij dawrat bi-markaz quwwat al-sawarikh bi-Wadi Al-Dawasir" [The Deputy Defense Minister Presides Over the Course Graduation in the Rocket Force's Center in Wadi Al-Dawasir], *Al-Jazira*, 16 June 2000, www.al-jazirah.com/2000/20000616/fr4.htm; and "Sumuw na'ib wazir al-difa."

[103] "Na'ib wazir al-difa yudashshin tariq Al-Amir Abd al-Rahman bayn Wadi Al-Dawasir wa'l-Daliya" [The Deputy Defense Minister Inaugurates the Prince Abd al-Rahman Road between Wadi Al-Dawasir wa'l-Daliya], *Al-Jazira*, 7

June 2001, www.al-jazirah.com/2001/20010607/s/ln1.htm.

[104] Fahd al-Ghaythi, "Al-Saudiya tastarid munjazatha askariyan bi-tadshin mabna li-quwwat al-sawarikh" [Saudi Arabia Displays Its Military Achievements with the Inauguration of the Rocket Force's Building], *Al-Iqtisadiya*, 3 March 2010, www.aleqt.com/2010/03/03/article_357900.html.

[105] "Al-Amir Abd al-Rahman yaftatih mabna tadrib markaz wa-madrasat quwwat al-sawarikh al-istratijiya" [Al-Amir Abd al-Rahman Inaugurates the Training Building at the SRF Center and School], *Al-Madina*, 11 July 2011, www.al-madina.com/node/314716.

[106] "Ra'is hay'at al-arkan yazur qaidat al-sawarikh al-istratijiya" [The Chief of Staff Visits a Strategic Rocket Base], *Al-Madina*, 30 January 2013, www.al-madina.com/printhtml/430132.

[107] "Khalid bin Sultan yuqallid al-fariq al-awwal Li An Dong wisam al-malik Abd al-Aziz min al-daraja al-mum-taza" [Khalid bin Sultan Awards Lieutenant General Li An Dong the King Abd al-Aziz Medal, Exceptional Class], *Al-Madina*, 6 October 2010, www.al-madina.com/print/267573.

[108] Salih al-Quthami, "Zhuhur sawarikh Riyah al-Sharq li-awwal marra tuthlij sudur al-saudiyin" [The Appearance of the East Wind Missiles for the First Time Delights the Saudis], *Sada* (Saudi Arabia), 29 April 2014, www/slaati.com/2014/04/29/p181530.html. (hereafter Al-Quthami, "Zhuhur sawarikh Riyah al-Sharq")

[109] Interview with Lieutenant General Salih al-Muhayya by Philip Finnegan, "Saudis Study Missile Buy to Replace Aging Arsenal," *Defense News*, (Annandale, VA), 12-23 March 1997, 42. (hereafter Al-Muhayya, "Saudis Study Missile Buy")

[110] Comment to "*The Telegraph*: Sawarikh saudiya musawwaba bi-ittijah Iran wa-Isra'il" [*The Telegraph*: Saudi Missiles Aimed at Iran and Israel], *Al-Marsad*, 16 July 2013, http://al-marsd.com/c-75082.

[111] Reported in Turki al-Suhayyil, "Al-Saudiya: Al-Amir Khalid bin Sultan yaftatih mansha'at al-sawarikh al-istrati-jiya" [Saudi Arabia: Prince Khalid bin Sultan Inaugurates a Strategic Rocket Facility], *Al-Sharq Al-Awsat*, 3 March 2010, www.aawsat.com/print.asp?did=559516&issueno=11418.

[112] Staff Major General Jar Allah al-Awit in his speech at the inauguration of the SRF's new headquarters, Fahd al-Ghaythi, "Al-Saudiya tastarid munjazatha askariyan bi-tadshin mabna li-quwwat al-sawarikh" [Saudi Arabia Displays Its Military Achievements with the Inauguration of the Rocket Force's Building], *Al-Iqtisadiya*, 3 March 2010, www.aleqt.com/2010/03/03/article_357900.html.

[113] "Al-Qaida bi'l-Hariq tulin an raghbatha fi isti'jar adwar wa-shuqaq fi Al-Huta wa'l-Hariq" [The Base at Al-Hariq Announces Its Desire to Rent Houses and Apartments in Al-Huta and Al-Hariq], *Al-Huta News*, 25 March 2011, www.alhota.net/news.php?action=show&id=2441.

[114] Said al-Thubayti, "Na'ib wazir al-difa yashhad hafl takhrij tullab kulliyat Al-Malik Abd-Allah" [The Deputy Minister of Defense Attends the Graduation Ceremony of the Students from King Abd-Allah Academy], *Al-Watan*, 3 June 2013, www.alwatan.com.sa/Politics/News_Detail.aspx?ArticleID=148172.

[115] Al-Hazimi, "Al-Amir Abd al-Rahman," the SRF web site, www.smf.gov.sa/help.htm; Saud al-Shibani, "Al-Muaddal al-amm li-jami al-dawrat 85.74%" [The Overall Average for All Courses Was 85.74%], *Al-Jazira*, 20 June 2004, www.al-jazirah.com/2004/20040620/ln41.htm; and Abd-Allah al-Hamdan, "Muhafizh Al-Dawasir yara hafl takhrij dubbat dawrat al-ta'ahil al-ilmi al-fanniya" [The Governor of Al-Dawasir Presides Over the Graduation Ceremony of Officers Graduating from the Professional Course for Scientific Training], *Al-Riyadh*, 15 January 2011, www.alriyadh.com/2011/01/15/article594724.html.

[116] Specific references to professional Saudi blogs are not provided in order to ensure the bloggers' privacy and security.

[117] Ronen Bergman, *Yediot Ahronot* (Tel Aviv), 27 March 2002, translated as "El-Sulayyil Missile Base – Saudi Desert," GlobalSecurity.org, www.globalsecurity.org/org/news/2002/020327-saudi.htm.

[118] Al-Muhayya, "Saudis Study Missile Buy," 3.

[119] Jonathan Scherck, *Patriot Lost*, (Los Angeles: The Author, 2010), 75, 96-7, passim. For an informed analysis of Scherck's claims, see Jeffrey Lewis, "Saudi Missile Claims," Arms Control Wonk blog, 8 June 2010, http://lewis.armscontrolwonk.com/archive/2761/china-and-saudi-bms.

[120] Sean O'Connor, "Saudi Ballistic Missile Site Revealed," *Jane's Defence Weekly* (London), 10 July 2013, https://janes.ihs.com. Also see the related analysis, "Secrets of the Sands: Saudi Arabia's Undisclosed Missile Site," *Jane's Intelligence Review* (London), 1 August 2013, http://search.proquest.com/docview/1399460080?accountid=1476.

[121] Jeffrey Lewis, "Saudi Arabia's Strategic Dyad," Arms Control Wonk blog, 15 July 2013, http://lewis.armscontrolwonk.com/archive/6688/saudi-arabias-strategic-dyad.

[122] Kimberly Van Dyke and Steve A. Yetiv, "Pakistan and Saudi Arabia: The Nuclear Nexus," *Journal of South Asian and Middle Eastern Studies* (Philadelphia), xxxiv, 4, Summer 2011, 68-84.

[123] "Al-Amir Sultan yanfi sayi Al-Saudiya li-imtilak silah nawawi" [Prince Sultan Denies That Saudi Arabia Is Seeking to Acquire Nuclear Weapons], *Al-Sharq Al-Awsat*, 5 August 1999, 1.

[124] A. Q. Khan, "My Services Are Well-known," *The News International* (Karachi), 6 October 2012, www.thenews.com.pk/PrintEdition.aspx?ID=136329&Cat=9&dt=12/7/2012.

[125] Jeff Stein, "The CIA Was Saudi Arabia's Personal Shopper," *Newsweek* (New York), 29 January 2014, http://mag.newsweek.com/2014/01/31/cia-saudi-arabias-personal-shopper.htm.

[126] Lewis, "Saudi Arabia's Strategic Dyad."

[127] For example, Abd al-Salam al-Rimawi, "Askari isra'ili: Al-Shita' al-qadim mawid qunbulat Iran al-nawawiya" [Israeli Military Man: Next Winter Is the Time for Iran's Nuclear Bomb], *Al-Riyadh*, 16 May 2009, based on *Haaretz* (Tel Aviv) article, www.alriyadh.com/429799, Reuters, "Taqrir duwali: Iran tutawwir sawarikh balistiya" [International Report: Iran Is Developing Ballistic Missiles], *Ukaz*, 18 May 2014, www.okaz.com.sa/new/Issues/20140518/Con20140518700107.htm, or Anthony Cordesman, "Al-Ittifaq al-nawawi la yunhi al-tahdidat al-iraniya li-duwal Majlis Al-Taawun" [A Nuclear Agreement Would Not End the Iranian Threats to the Gulf Cooperation Council Countries], *Al-Madina*, 18 April 2014, www.al-madina.com/node/525481.

[128] "Al-Saudiya tutawwir sawarikh balistiya fattaka wa-tashtari rajimat ifriqiya" [Saudi Arabia Is Developing Lethal Ballistic Missiles and Is Buying [South] African Launchers], report from *Naba' News* (Sanaa), reproduced in *Jazan News* (Jazan, Saudi Arabia), 13 March 2010, www.jazannews.org/news.php?action=show&id=2836.

[129] Ibid.

[130] Sami Said Habib, "Qira'a fi tasrihat Al-Faysal" [An Analysis of [Turki] Al-Faysal's Statements], *Al-Madina*, 10 December 2011, www.al-madina.com/print/343867.

[131] "Al-Tarsana al-sarukhiya bi'l-Mamlaka Al-Arabiya Al-Saudiya" [The Missile Arsenal in the Kingdom of Saudi Arabia], Arar forum (Arar, Saudi Arabia), 14 December 2012, www.alshmaly.net/vb/showthread.php?=86914.

[132] Husayn Ayyub, "Putin li-Bandar: Tatlubun sawarikh balistiya ila Misr li-darb Iran!" [Putin to Bandar: You Are Requesting Ballistic Missiles for Egypt in Order Strike Iran!], *Al-Safir* (Beirut), 22 January 2014, www.assafir.com.

[133] Sami Said Habib, "Taqniyat al-sawarikh: al-mahzhur raqm athnayn ala al-umma al-islamiya" [Missile Technology: The Number Two Prohibition for the Islamic Umma], Saudi Election website, 19 September 2006, http://saudi-election.com/ar/forum/showthread.php?t=23892.

[134] Sami Said Habib, "Taqniyat al-sawarikh: al-mahzhur raqm athnayn ala al-umma al-islamiya" [Missile Technology: The Number Two Prohibition for the Islamic Umma], Saudi Election website, 19 September 2006, http://saudi-election.com/ar/forum/showthread.php?t=23892; and Sami Said Habib, "Harb al-sawarikh al-qadima" [The Coming Missile War], Wahat al-Arab website, 8 September 2007, www.wahatalarab.com/ap/showArticle.aspx?Art_ID=57788&Replypos=2.

[135] Al-Umari, "Dawafi imtilak al-qudrat", 13, 15.

[136] Quoted in Simpson, *The Prince*, 166.

[137] "Yak nas rozzbroyuyut' SShA" [How the United States Disarms Us], Teksty.org.ua (Ukraine), 22 December 2010, http://texty.org.ua; and "Ukraina vvyazalas' v skandal s raketami dlya Saudovskoiy Aravii" [Ukraine Was Involved in Scandal over Missiles for Saudi Arabia], *Segodnya* (Kiev), 8 December 2011, www.segodnya.ua.

[138] "Tullab al-jamia al-mutamayyizun yazurun al-jamiat al-kuriya al-janubiya" [Excpetional University Students Visit South Korean Universities], King Saud University website, 15 February 2011, www.cksu.com/vb/showthread.php?t=269573.

[139] "Sumuw na'ib wazir al-difa yazur majmuat sharikat Poly al-siniya" [His Highness the Deputy Minister of Defense Visits the Chinese Poly Group Corporation], Al-Riyadh, 4 April 2013, www.alriyadh.com/2013/04/04/article823189.html.

[140] "Ra'is al-mukhabarat al-saudiya akkad ann al-nawawi al-isra'ili yuthir sibaq tasalluh" [The Head of Saudi Intelligence Asserted That Israel's Nuclear Weapons Would Spur an Arms Race], Al-Arabiya TV (Abu Dhabi, UAE), 9 December 2006, transcript at www.alarabiya.net/articles/2006/12/09/29744.html.

[141] Reported in Chemi Shalev, "Dennis Ross: Saudi King Vowed to Obtain Nuclear Bomb after Iran" *Haaretz*, 30 May 2012, www.haaretz.com/news/diplomacy-defense/dennis-ross-saudi-king-vowed-to-obtain-nuclear-bomb-after-iran-1.433294.

[142] Talal Salih Bannan, "Al-Arab bayn kammashat al-rub al-nawawi!" [The Arabs between the Pincers of Nuclear Terror!], *Ukaz*, 2 April 2006, www.okaz.com.sa/okaz/osf/20060402/PrinCon200604026920.htm. (hereafter Bannan, "Al-Arab")

[143] Adnan Kamil Salah, "Al-Qadiya al-iraniya bi-ru'ya arabiya muwahhada" [The Iranian Case from a United Arab Perspective], *Al-Madina*, 7 January 2010, www.al-madina.com/print/213010.

[144] "Wast mazid min al-tawatturat wa'l-daght al-sarukh al-irani Shihab-3 yadkhul al-khidma" [Amid Increasing Tensions and Pressure the Iranian Shihab-3 Missile Enters Service], *Majallat Kulliyat Al-Malik Khalid Al-Askariya*, December 2003, 90-93.

[145] Izzat Muhammad Ali, "Al-Sarukh al-irani Shihab-3 yadkhul al-khidma" [The Shihab-3 Iranian Missile Enters Service], *Majallat Kulliyat Al-Malik Khalid Al-Askariya*, December 2002, 90.

[146] For example, Muhammad Ali al-Buraydi, "Sawarikh Iran wa-qitat Al-Khalij" [Iran's Missiles and the Gulf's Scaredy Cats], *Al-Sharq* (Najran), 5 February 2013, www.alsharq.net.sa/2013/02/05/707819.

[147] Adnan Kamil Salah, "Wad Iran wa-Isra'il taht mizhallat naz silah nawawi wahida" [Placing Iran and Israel under a Single Nuclear Disarmament Umbrella], *Al-Madina*, 17 December 2013, www.al-madina.com/printhtml/498590.

[148] Mustafa al-Tarhuni, "Muhadathat Iran al-nawawiya wa-aqabat al-sawarikh" [Iran's Nuclear Negotiations and the Missile Obstacle], *Al-Madina*, 13 April 2014, www.al-madina.com/printhml/524239, and Jasir Abd al-Aziz al-Jasir, "Al-Uyun al-gharbiya tughammad an al-ghubar al-nawawi al-irani" [The West's Eyes Are Blinded by Iran's Nuclear Dust], *Al-Jazira*, 23 February 2014, www.al-jazirah.com/2014/20140223/du6.htm.

[149] Major General Husam Suwaylim (Retired), "Ahdaf Iran al-siyasiya wa'l-istratijiya wa-asalib tahqiqha," [Iran's Political and Strategic Objectives and the Methods to Achieve Them], *Al-Haras Al-Watani*, part 1, August 2011, 33-34, 36. This is the Saudi National Guard's professional journal.

[150] "Nass kalimat al-amir Saud al-Faysal wazir al-kharijiya al-saudiya" [The Text of the Speech by Prince Saud al-Faysal, Saudi Arabia's Foreign Minister], *Al-Sharq Al-Awsat*, 7 January 2009, www.aawsat.com/print.asp?did=501885&issueno=10998.

[151] Al-Imam, "Al-amn al-qawmi."

[152] Abd al-Rahman al-Rashid, "Isra'il tashinn harb Al-Khalij al-muqbila!" [Israel Will Spark the Next Gulf War!], *Al-Sharq Al-Awsat*, 18 April 2013, www.aawsat.com.

[153] Yusuf Kamil Khattab, "Qira'a fi al-malaff al-nawawi al-isra'ili" [An Analysis of the Israeli Nuclear Program],

Majallat Kulliyat Al-Malik Khalid Al-Askariya, 1 December 2002, 62.

[154] For example, Deputy Minister of Culture Salih al-Namla, "Pakistan wa-tajrubat al-rad al-nawawi" [Pakistan and the Experience of Nuclear Deterrence], *Al-Riyadh*, 12 June 2002, p. 32.

[155] Abd al-Jalil al-Marhun, "Man yarfud taqlis al-asliha al-hujumiya?" [Who Is Refusing to Reduce Offensive Weapons?], *Al-Riyadh*, 15 January 2010, www.al-riyadh.com/2010/01/15/article489828.html.

[156] Al-Umari, "Dawafi imtilak al-qudrat," 15.

[157] Interview with Prince Turki al-Faysal, BBC Arabic News (London), 8 July 2011, www.youtube.com/watch?=Kfw.R7j4-HwZO.

[158] Najib al-Khunayzi, "Hal hunak mawqif irani jadid?" [Is There a New Iranian Position?], *Ukaz*, 6 October 2013, www.okaz.com.sa/new/Issues/20131006/PrinCon20131006644868.htm., Ayman al-Hammad, "Hisabat gharbiya is-tratijiya qad tuid 'shurti Al-Khalij'" [Western Strategic Calculations May Return the "Gulf Policeman"], *Al-Riyadh*, On-line, Internet, 26 October 2013, www.alriyadh.com/2013/10/26/article878682.html, and Ibrahim al-Uthaymin, "Li-madha turid Iran al-taqarub ma Amrika?" [Why Does Iran Want a Rapprochement with America?], *Al-Yawm*, 18 October 2013, www.alyaum.com/News/art/999216.html.

[159] Mutlaq Saud al-Mtiri, "Al-Ayn al-thalitha wa'l-tafawud ma Tihran" [The Third Eye and Negotiating with Tehran], *Al-Riyadh*, On-line, Internet, 23 September 2013, available from www.al-riyadh.com/2013/09/23/article869831.html, Muhammad al-Uthaym, "Obama muharwilan" [Obama Is in a Rush], *Al-Iqtisadiya*, 2 October 2013, www.aleqt.com/2013/10/02/article_790042.print, Mutlaq Saud Al-Mtiri, "Man tughatta bi'l-amrikan aryan" [He Who Uses the Americans as Clothing Is Naked], *Al-Riyadh*, 2 October 2013, www.alriyadh.com/2013/10/02/article872192.html, Yusuf al-Kuwaylit, "Safaqat qad taksibha Iran" [Deals in Which Iran Could Be the Winner], *Al-Riyadh*, 25 September 2013, www.alriyadh.com/2013/09/25/article870345.html, and Hamad bin Abd-Allah al-Luhaydan, "Al-Yawm al-watani 83 quwwa wa-izza wa-istidad" [The 83rd National Day: Power, Pride, and Pre-paredness], *Anba'kum*, 20 September 2013, www.anbacom.com/print.php?action=print&m=articlesm&id=17541. (hereafter Al-Luhaydan, "Al-Yawm al-watani").

[160] For example, Mutlaq Saud al-Mtiri, "Musku tuarri marra thaniya al-daf al-amriki" [Moscow Exposes Once Again America's Weakness], *Al-Riyadh*, 8 March 2014, www.alriyadh.com/916328.

[161] The Political Editor, "Al-Alaqat bayn Al-Riyadh wa-Washintun … jawhar al-haqiqa wa-tafasil al-marhala" [Relations between Riyadh and Washington: The Essence of the State of Affairs and the Details about This Phase], *Al-Riyadh*, 25 October 2013, www.alriyadh.com/2013/10/25/article878375.html.

[162] Prince Mohammed bin Nawaf bin Abdulaziz al-Saud, "Saudi Arabia Will Go It Alone," *New York Times*, 17 October 2013, www.nytimes.com/2013/12/18/opinion/saudi-arabia-will-go-it-alone.html?_r=0.

[163] Abd al-Rahman al-Turayri, "Al-Khalij arabi am farisi?" [The Gulf: Arab or Persian?], *Al-Iqtisadiya* (Jeddah), 23 August 2011, www.aleqt.com/2011/08/23/article_572330.print.

[164] Al-Umari, "Dawafi imtilak al-qudrat," 12-13.

[165] Bannan, "Al-Arab."

[166] Al-Umari, "Dawafi imtilak al-qudrat," 15.

[167] Ibid, 13.

[168] Muhammad al-Ghunayyim, "Sayf Abd-Allah risalat quwwa wa-rd wa-itmi'nan" [The Sword of Abd Allah Is a Message of Strength, Deterrence, and Reassurance], *Al-Riyadh*, 2 May 2014, www.alriyadh.com/932047.html.

[169] "Kulluna Sayf Abd-Allah" [We Are All the Sword of Abd-Allah], *Al-Watan*, 30 April 2014, www.alwatan.com.sa/Editors_Note/Default.aspx.

[170] Zuhayr al-Harithi, "Sayf Abd-Allah: Al-Risala wasalat" [The Sword of Abd-Allah: The Message Was Received], *Al-Riyadh*, 6 May 2014, www.alriyadh.com/933200. (hereafter Al-Harithi, "Sayf Abd-Allah")

[171] Nayif al-Asimi, "Sayf Abd-Allah risala saudiya li-quwa al-sharr" [The Sword of Abd-Allah Is a Saudi Message to the Forces of Evil], *Al-Watan*, 29 April 2014, www.alwatan.com.sa/Local/News_Detail.aspx?ArticleID=186428&CategoryID=5.

[172] Nayif al-Asimi, "Sayf Abd-Allah ilan salam wa-itmi'nan" [The Sword of Abd-Allah: A Declaration of Peace and Reassurance], *Al-Watan*, 30 April 2014, www.alwatan.com.sa/Local/News_Detail.aspx?ArticleID=186511&CategoryID=5.

[173] Bandar al-Dawshi, "Abr al-sarukh al-balisti Al-Saudiya tafrud halat al-samt ala al-mutarabbisin" [By Means of the Ballistic Missiles Saudi Arabia Silenced Those Who Are Lurking], *Sabq*, 30 April 2014, http://sabq.org/yGYfde. (hereafter Al-Dawshi, "Abr al-sarukh al-balisti")

[174] Yasir al-Ghaslan, "Kaff Sayf Abd-Allah" [The Slap of the Sword of Abd-Allah], *Al-Watan*, 1 May 2014, www.alwatan.com.sa/Articles/Detail.aspx?ArticleId=21160.

[175] Muhammad Hasan Mufti, "Sayf Abd-Allah risala li-man yahummuh al-amr" [The Sword of Abd-Allah Was a Message for the Intended Parties], *Ukaz*, 6 May 2014, www.okaz.com.sa/news/issues/20140506/PrinCon20140506697493.htm. (hereafter Mufti, "Sayf Abd-Allah")

[176] Al-Dawshi, "Abr al-sarukh al-balisti," and Al-Harithi, "Sayf Abd-Allah."

[177] Al-Harithi, "Sayf Abd-Allah."

[178] "Kulluna Sayf Abd-Allah" [We Are All the Sword of Abd-Allah], *Al-Watan*, 30 April 2014, www.alwatan.com.sa/Editors_Note/Default.aspx.

[179] Mansur al-Shihri, "Ard askari yuzhhir qudrat fa'iqa li-taslih quwwatna barran wa-bahran wa-jawwan" [A Military Parade Reveals the Great Power of the Weaponry of Our Land, Sea, and Air Forces], *Ukaz*, 30 April 2014, www.okaz.com.sa/new/mobilenew/20140430/Con20140430696093.htm.

[180] Mansur al-Shihri, "Riyah Al-Sharq risalat itmi'nan li'l-shab wa-tahdhir li'l-aduww" [The East Wind Is a Message of Reassurance for the Population and a Warning to the Enemy], *Ukaz*, 1 May 2014, www.okaz.com.sa/new/issues/20140501/PrinCon20140501696350.htm.

[181] Makarim Subhi Batarji, "La ahad yastahin bi'l-quwwa" [No One Can Humiliate Someone Who Has Power], *Ukaz*, 1 May 2014, www.okaz.com.sa/new/issues/20140501/PrinCon20140501696406.htm.

[182] Al-Hammad, "Madha bad."

[183] Mufti, "Sayf Abd-Allah."

[184] Ibid.

[185] For example, "Li-awwal marra sawarikh Riyah al-Sharq al-qadira ala haml ru'us nawawiya bi munawarat 'Sayf Abd-Allah'" [For the First Time in the Sword of Abd-Allah Exercise the East Wind Missiles That Are Nuclear-Capable] , *Tawasul* (Riyadh), 30 April 2014, http://twasul.info/55974, "Al-Salmi: Sayf Abd-Allah tabath rasa'il mutaaddida" [Al-Salmi: Sword of Abd-Allah Send Multiple Messages], *Arkan* (Saudi Arabia), 30 April 2014, www.arkan-news.com/?p=1556, Al-Quthami, "Zhuhur sawarikh Riyah al-Sharq," or "Al-Saudiya tastakhdim silah jadid li-awwal marra fi munawarat askariya" [Saudi Arabia Uses New Weapons for the First Time in Military Exercises], *Al-Rajul* (Saudi Arabia), 1 May 2014, www.arrajol.com.

[186] Al-Dawshi, "Abr al-sarukh al-balisti."

[187] Ahmad Ghallab, "Al-Saudiya tastarid quwwatha amam al-alam bi-Sayf Abd-Allah" [Saudi Arabia Displays Its Power to the World with the Sword of Abd-Allah Exercise], *Al-Hayat* (Saudi edition), 29 April 2014, http://alhayat.com/Articles/20544569.

[188] Viktor Krest'yaninov, "Rakety saudovskikh vakhkhabitov dostanut do nashei strany" [The Saudi Wahhabis' Missiles Can Reach Our Country], *Argumenty Nedeli* (Moscow), 6 February 2014, http://argumenti.ru/politics/n424/317243.

About the Author

Norman Cigar is a Research Fellow at the Marine Corps University, Quantico, Virginia, from which he retired recently as Director of Regional Studies and the Minerva Research Chair. Previously, he had also taught at the Marine Corps Command and Staff College and at the Marine Corps School of Advanced Warfighting. In an earlier assignment, he spent seven years as a senior political-military analyst in the Pentagon, where he was responsible for the Middle East in the Office of the Army's Deputy Chief of Staff for Intelligence, and supported the Secretary of the Army, the Chief of Staff of the Army, and Congress with intelligence. He also represented the Army on national-level intelligence issues in the interagency intelligence community. During the Gulf War, he was the Army's senior political-military intelligence staff officer on the Desert Shield/Desert Storm Task Force.

He is the author of numerous works on politics and security issues dealing with the Middle East and the Balkans, and has been a consultant at the International Criminal Tribunal for the former Yugoslavia at the Hague. He has also taught at the National Intelligence University and was a Visiting Fellow at the Institute for Conflict Analysis & Resolution, George Mason University. Among his writings are *Libya's Nuclear Disarmament: Lessons and Implications for Nuclear Proliferation*; *Saddam's Nuclear Vision: An Atomic Shield and Sword for Conquest*; and *Thinking about Nuclear Power in Post-Saddam Iraq*.

Dr. Cigar holds a DPhil from Oxford (St Antony's College) in Middle East History and Arabic; an M.I.A. from the School of International and Public Affairs and a Certificate from the Middle East Institute, Columbia University; and an M.S.S.I. from the National Intelligence University. He has studied and traveled widely in the Middle East.

Acknowledgements

The author would like to express his gratitude to the Earhart Foundation for a generous grant which made possible the research and writing of this study. The views expressed here are those of the author and do not reflect the official policy or position of the U. S. Government, the Department of Defense, the U. S. Marine Corps, Marine Corps University, or the Earhart Foundation.

Saudi Arabia's Strategic Rocket Force
The Silent Service

Norman Cigar

This monograph deals with Saudi Arabia's Strategic Rocket Force—the "silent force" because it receives far less publicity than the country's other armed services. The study addressed the decision for the original acquisition of the surface-to-surface missiles (SSM), the doctrine and employment parameters developed, and the current status of the missile force, and forecasts future potential developments and prospect. In particular, the study examines Saudi Arabia's experience with deterrence doctrine, command and control practices, force structure, and considerations of domestic, regional, and international factors with respect to the SSM, which can also provide significant insights into Saudi thinking that could also be applied to understanding that country's behavior in relation to a potential nuclear option at some time in the future. The Strategic Rocket Force has continued to develop over the years, including a reported upgrading of the missile systems in the Saudi arsenal. Any study of SSM in Saudi Arabia must include addressing the issue from Saudi Arabia's own perspective if one is to understand the dynamics which have shaped policy and are likely to indicate future behavior and the study relies heavily on Saudi sources for information. Among the study's conclusions are that Saudi Arabia will continue to view its SSM as a key component of its force structure, with a primary emphasis on deterrence; the apparent recent upgrade in the SSM force, if confirmed, is an additional indication that Saudi Arabia is likely to consider following suit if Iran succeeds in developing a nuclear capability—almost assuredly by direct acquisition of a ready-made capability from abroad, and very likely from Pakistan—especially given the Saudi view of SSM and nuclear weapons as an interrelated package; and that although Saudi Arabia intends its SSMs to have a stabilizing effect in the region by deterring potential aggression and adventurism, such upgraded arsenals also open the way for further arms races and increased regional tensions.